POOR LENIN'S ALMANAC

POOR LENIN'S ALMANAC

Perverse Leftist Proverbs for Modern Life

By Bruce Walker

Outskirts Press, Inc.
Denver, Colorado

Outskirts Press, Inc.
http://www.outskirtspress.com

ISBN: 978-1-4327-5682-6

Outskirts Press and the "OP" logo are trademarks belonging to Outskirts Press, Inc.

PRINTED IN THE UNITED STATES OF AMERICA

Preface

Proverbs, maxims, and sayings have been part and parcel of human experience everywhere as long as we have had language. We do not know the origin of some of these proverbs, but we do know that as early as Aesop and his Fables and as early as the Bible and its Proverbs, men have boiled down wisdom into brief and clear expressions.

"The early bird catches the worm" doubtless has counterparts in many cultures and in many languages. "All that glitters is not gold" is another proverb which rings true in our history at many places in many times and in countless situations and the same for "The apple does not fall far from the tree."

Proverbs are meant for ordinary people. Proverbs are intended to express common sense. Proverbs are not ideological: they reflect preserved wisdom. These quick references for living are generalizations. The early bird does not always catch the worm, but it is more likely to do so. All that glitters is not gold, but gold glitters brightly. Some apples do fall a distance from the tree trunk, but most do not.

Although general, proverbs are grounded in life. One never hears proverbs like "Rudeness makes true friends" or "Mud pies are the best deserts." Simple words which have grown from a mature observation of life into a brief analogy of wisdom are essentially and generally correct. This means that proverbs are "conservative" in the ordinary, non-ideological sense of the word (proverbs conserve accumulated wisdom) but it also means that proverbs are "conservative" in the usual ideological sense (proverbs do not believe we can make Heaven on Earth.) Proverbs do not try to change basic human behavior. Proverbs, rather, try to describe basic human behavior. Proverbs are not regulatory but cautionary. Proverbs imply personal choice, a measure of human freedom, an assumed range of liberty, and personal responsibility.

Proverbs require faith in the past. Those who believe history means nothing gain nothing from proverbs. But these sorts of people are fools. Our "now" is in the past as soon as it is spoken, but the truth of proverbs exists in the past, present, and future all at once. If we ran the cosmos, proverbs would be meaningless, but because we run almost nothing, not even the course of our own lives except in limited ways, proverbs matter.

The ideological Left (which I have described, along with its identical twins on the mythical "Far Right," at some extremes of a fanciful ideological spectrum, as simply "Sinisterism") has no use for the collective wisdom of grandfathers, field hands, housewives and long dead scribes. As Orwell notes so brilliantly in *1984*, the very meaning of language must be changed, the very vestiges of historical experience must be continually destroyed and recreated, if those who want wisdom are to be permanently silenced.

That, of course, is precisely what Marxists, Nazis, modern "Progressives," Fascists and all these interchangeable goons of cognition and knowledge want: they want not just to disarm our bodies but to mutilate our minds and to despoil our souls. As long as a mother's recorded caution about crying over spilt milk lives in human thought, Sinisterists cannot gain the only thing that Sinisterists ever really want: power; power over our lives; power over our minds; power over our souls.

It is with this knowledge that I write "Poor Lenin's Almanac," a parody of Ben Franklin's famous book of ordinary truths. Many of my "proverbs" are not proverbs *per se*, but rather phrases and expressions in modern culture which most of us have heard at one time or another. Some are based on the titles of popular music. Others are corruptions of words from American politics. All are intended to expose, by perverted proverbs, the griminess, the emptiness, the mendacity, and the meanness of those who would rule us.

Lenin has gotten much better press from historians and pundits than he deserves. Stalin, many apologists for the long nightmare that was Soviet Russia believe, was the real villain. No: Lenin was just as bloodthirsty, just as vicious, and just as dishonest as Stalin. He ordered the execution of children. He fathered the Cheka (precursor not only of the KGB, but also the Gestapo.) He made slimy political deals in order to preserve his power. Lenin was as bad as bad gets.

Lenin, more than anyone else, is the father of that awful mess of modern muddle which we call "progressive" or "liberal" or "politically correct." No one looks back with much nostalgia to Stalin and most people have only a vague idea of what Marx really preached (the racism of Marx, for example, passes unnoticed.) Lenin, however, wrote much, said much, and laid the practical groundwork for much of the mischief in the world today. So Vladimir Ilyich, not Stalin or Marx or some modern Leftist, gets the "credit" for the perverse collection of modern proverbs in this book.

Contents

I am living in a political world and I am a political girl

Madonna, when she used to be an entertainer rather than a recreational adopter of children, sang "I am living in a material world, and I am a material girl." Money mattered, her song said. Love did not. But it is not money *per se* which matters to Poor Lenin. He wants power. Once, in the misty past when our Founding Fathers tried to create a polity in which the power of government over our lives was limited to essential tasks, money meant more.

Nowadays, getting political power is often the easiest path to wealth, rather than wealth being the easiest path to political power. Look at all the rich politicians. Don't you wonder where they got their wealth? Look at all the wealth squeezed out of government by "friends" of politicians, who use tax dollars like juice restaurants use oranges and grapefruit. But the connection between politics over money is even stronger.

To get ahead in the world, it is necessary to be politically correct. Political views, more than talent, should determine – in Poor Lenin's mind – who is a star in the entertainment world and who is not. So, a great actor like Charlton Heston, whose inimitable brilliance filled the greatest roles that film could find, found it harder and harder to find work in the ghetto of the politically incorrect in Hollywood. Meanwhile hare-brained celebrities who mouth the goo-goos of the elites gain *entre* into the offices of television, music, and film executives.

There is a vast universe of human talent which lies fallow, unplowed, unused because it would be "politically incorrect." And because political correctness requires the same sort of bizarre twists and turns that the party line did in the old Communist Party, being politically correct means ignoring a possible rapist in the White House who is accused by several different women of terrorizing them (because this man is politically correct) but demanding that a Supreme Court nominee be defeated when a single woman makes utterly unsubstantiated allegation of sexual harassment.

Being politically correct means that poetry is good or bad based solely on its political perspective. It means that art is great or lousy based upon its political theme. It means that music is glorious or ghastly depending upon the militancy towards traditional values of its lyrics. Being politically correct means that every celebrity, every fiction writer, every scientist with an unusual theory, every charitable event, everything at all, in fact, in public life must bear the imprimatur of the "Party Line."

It means, in other words, that the true arts die a slow death of starvation. It means, in other words, that music gradually degrades into puerile tirades or sappy baby talk. It means, in other words, that the public life has only a political component and nothing else. Entertainment, art, philosophy – all must conform to the politics of Poor Lenin.

Beyond that, it means that any real inquiry for truth must first pass, as a camel, through the needle's eye of political correctness. Global warming becomes true, and must be true at every government agency and in every corporate office and in every university department, because politics demands that the planet must be warming. If the party – or the hive – tomorrow demanded that pigs must be able to fly, then Poor Lenin and his entourage would solemnly wait on the White House lawn for the first porcine flight to pass overhead. To paraphrase the ancient Greeks "Ideology is the measure of all things." We are living in a political world, and life will never get better until we shed that burden.

·

Birds of a feather must vote together

Democracy, Churchill warned us, is the worst form of government, except for all the rest. The virtues of democracy are not those we often suppose. People, especially people huddled around "interest groups," have no right to take the sovereign power of democracy and use that to get what they want. Democracy is intended to protect all of us from excessive government. The notion that votes in a democracy should be used to empower our race, our sex, or our faith is the same sort of nasty bigotry which Hitler employed to come to power in Germany. If people truly believe that this is the purpose of democracy, then this proverb justifies Aryan politics or White Supremacy politics as much as it justifies Black politics.

Poor Lenin strives to create a democracy full of frightened, angry tribes of voters. He does not want an electorate composed of millions of independent and individual voters who are jurors judging on the truthfulness, competence, and impartiality of government. Poor Lenin wants us to vote if we are black for a black (or for someone who advocates the interests of black people) and for women to vote for women (or for someone who advocates the interests of women) and so on.

Our Constitution, our Bill of Rights, the Equal Protection Clause of the Fourteenth Amendment (considered vital to civil rights), and our idea of blind justice all enshrine just the opposite idea: We are not supposed to exercise our civil and political rights to gain special advantages for our "group." Christians are not supposed to vote as a bloc to promote Christianity at the expense of Judaism. Men are not supposed to vote as a bloc to make laws more favorable to men than to women. White people are not supposed to use their vote to maintain "White Power."

When jurors in criminal trials stop looking at the evidence and start looking at the skin color, the religion, or the gender of the defendant, we no longer have a system of justice but a regime of social justice. That means white juries let violent members of the Ku Klux Klan walk free and black juries have let murderers like O.J. Simpson escape justice in the pursuit of "social justice" (or, rather, injustice.)

In a democracy, when voters look at candidates and policies to see what is in it for them, then the whole idea of the "general welfare" dies. If a coalition of different flocks of birds can be combined into a majority – if voters regard themselves as birds of a flock instead of voters with a moral responsibility to all their countrymen, without regard to race, creed or gender – then there is nothing to prevent the majority from becoming a savage, greedy, bigoted tyranny. There is also nothing to prevent an opposing coalition, when it cobbles together its own selfish majority, from abusing power just as badly.

Democracy works when birds stop looking at their feathers and start looking at their consciences. We are each a "juror" and those in power are always on trial. Our duty is not to see what is in politics for us. Our duty is to use our vote and our voice to see that our political system is fair, neutral, and just. Voters are not supposed to vote to elect men who will provide special help to them. In fact, when powerful people use government to help themselves, we rightly consider that to be political corruption.

If the League of Brown Eyed Voters organized into a voting bloc and adopted a program like this: "Brown eyed voters perform the vast majority of the important, hard work that has made our nation strong, yet, on average, blue eyed voters and green eyed voters have more money and more education than brown eyed voters. Vote your brown-eyed interests! Vote to protect the rights of exploited brown eyed voters!" would that not be just the short of "interest politics" so favored by Poor Lenin? If one should feel morally obligated to support the policies and candidates championing one skin color, why not eye color too? Indeed, why not hair color? Is it true blondes have more fun? Well, they would not if blondes were confined to a weak voting bloc while the proletariat brunettes, the oppressed majority, used its power of the vote to rectify that bias in favor of blue eyed blondes or green eyed redheads. Birds of a feather, color, and every other difference should vote together! (Or so says Poor Lenin.)

A victim in need is a vote indeed

Poor Lenin cannot live without miserable people. Whatever you imagine about your life, Poor Lenin can convince you that you are really a victim. Are you a woman? Then you are a victim. Are you black or brown or yellow? Then you are a victim. Are you handicapped? Then you are a victim. Do you have a child with special needs? Then you are a victim. Are you a child? Then you are a victim. Are you rather old? Then you are a victim.

Victims, according to Poor Lenin, are not people with problems to overcome. Victims are deserving people. Victims are wronged people. Victims have special rights. This philosophy of Poor Lenin is radically different than what being a victim has meant throughout human history. When Mongols razed cities, the inhabitants were victims. When Roman armies marched, victims were left in the wake. When the Aztecs needed for human hearts to placate their savage gods, victims were captured in war and brought before the altar for sacrifice.

These victims did not do anything ennobling. These victims might have been villains as well as victims. The cities razed by Mongols might have conquered other cities, if they could. Were German soldiers who were hammered by Allied warplanes also victims? Yes...and? We all suffer in life and we all in time die. Are we all victims? Pretty much. Whose "victimhood" counts more? We are not God. We do not know.

It is also an important fact that victims may be the principal reason for their problems in life, like alcoholics or drug abusers. Young men who join gangs are more likely to be the victim of violence than studious boys who come home and study at night. None of this diminishes the fact that injured and savaged people are victims, but it changes the character of their victimhood from the sort of nobility that Poor Lenin invents into a sort of circumstantial test: the moral status of every victim must be judged individually.

In the real world, throughout human history, there was nothing particularly honorable about being a victim. It was unfortunate. It might – it often should – induce pity and charity from compassionate people. But it was not the source of human goodness. Indeed, it was largely disconnected from human goodness.

Only masochists want to continue being "victims," and only sadists want victims to stay victims. Well, Poor Lenin views sadism and masochism as nonjudgmental versions of alternative lifestyles. Most importantly, the only thing in Poor Lenin's life that matters is what makes him a tin pot deity. By convincing groups of people that they are eternal victims and that he is their local god, Poor Lenin can persuade people to always support him – not just with their votes, but with their voices, their anger, and their curses against the eternal enemy.

A VICTIM IN NEED

So, Poor Lenin can persuade many blacks that white people were born into this universe as special demons sent to torment blacks. Forget that Republicans and conservative Christians were the first supporters of civil rights for blacks and that the Ku Klux Klan was the terrorist arm of the Democrat Party. Republicans who are conservative Christians are always and forever enemies of black folk.

Forget, if you are a feminist, that women were given the right to vote because a majority of men thought this was the moral and honorable course of action. Forget that if men really were a secret and suppressive cabal they would not have given women the right to vote. If men had the wealth, the legal rights, the physical power, the exclusive right to vote, and equal numbers with women, why, on Earth, would men give up all that power unless men loved their wives, loved their mothers, loved their sisters, loved their daughters, and viewed women as essentially noble and good?

Nothing in Poor Lenin's grand volume of victims and victimizers really makes any sense at all. But, of course, it is not intended to make sense in the same way as a math equation, a law of science, or a paragraph of intelligent text makes sense. Victims, to Poor Lenin, must at all cost remain victims. So when blacks get "uppity" like Thomas Sowell, Clarence Thomas, or Alan Keyes, then it is not enough just to stop these blacks who proclaim "Guess what? I am not a victim! I am a success story!" Those blacks who speak in the public forum must recant and recite the catechism of Poor Lenin or they must be lynched.

If a woman is conservative and vocal, then she is fair game for all of the malicious mischief which feminists would seriously proclaim as vicious misogyny if used against any other woman anywhere – except a conservative woman speaking her mind. How often does NOW speak up in defense of Ann Coulter, the most successful polemicist in modern society? (They hate her and they never, ever, object to anything done to her.) How often did NOW complain about the personal attacks on Sarah Palin or the absurd ethical charges leveled against her? Never.

Most of all, Poor Lenin wants blacks, women, and whoever else feels impotent, abused, and despised to always feel that way. The worst thing possible for Poor Lenin is for victims to stop feeling like victims. These victims are the milk cows of Poor Lenin's herds. He needs their wretchedness and he will do everything in his power to keep them that way.

Everyone, ultimately, is a victim. Poor Lenin's good friend Hitler rose to power on the wings of the victimization of the German people. All myths of eternal victimhood have a grain of truth. Yes, reparations imposed by the Versailles Treaty were unfair to the German people. Yes, German-speaking territories were unfairly kept outside of Germany. Yes, some of the claims of the Nazis had some moral weight. But, of course, it did not matter that the Allies were willing to rectify many past wrongs. Hitler portrayed Germans as eternal victims, whose true greatness was only hidden because of a cast of eternal villains. Who were these villains? Jews, yes, of course – remember Emanuel Goldstein, the eternal villain in Orwell's 1984? The rich were hated by the Nazis. Christians? They were the ultimate enemy, according to much Nazi propaganda.

The elevation of victimhood as a holy rite of an intolerant religion ultimately means that those who actually were to blame in the past for some wrongs are ignored, while those who actually were good to the victims become convenient villains. So German Jews, who were intensely patriotic, became villains. Businessmen who helped Germany through the roughest days of the Weimar Republic were capitalist oppressors. Christians, who wished most of all for a world of peace, became the apostles of German weakness.

Christians and Republicans were the greatest champions of black people when there was no profit in it. So who are the "champions" of black people now? Notional Christians who preach hatred rather than love are the spokesmen of "black America" and Democrats, the political party of the Ku Klux Klan, are the leaders of "black America."

Those told again and again that they were victims become, over time, villains. Victimhood grants (or pretends to grant) a license to do evil for the sake of the greater good. After all, I am a victim, right? And as long as the

POOR LENIN'S ALMANAC

Kulak, the Jew or the Republican keeps me down – and Poor Lenin is always very good about telling me just who is keeping me down – then anything I do to those "oppressors" is moral and right. Poor Lenin told me so, and he is (sob) my only true friend.

You can only judge a book by its color

How do we know if a person is honest? How do we know if a person is good? How do we know if a person is competent? Once upon a time, in a land far away, a man said: "I dream of the day when men will be judged by the content of their character and not by the color of their skin…" Dr. King had the right idea, but Poor Lenin just ignored his advice.

Poor Lenin does not dream of that day at all. Color, gender, language, everything that distinguishes us must be preserved in the hothouse of Poor Lenin. Qualifications on a job form must include the most important qualification: what is your race or national origin? When white men were accused of rape by a black woman, it did not take the faculty at Duke University long to render its verdict. "White men? Black woman?" Obviously the white men are guilty. Indeed, even if they are innocent, they are guilty. Moreover, because the Lacrosse Team was guilty, that served as more proof that whites are guilty in general.

When a "civil rights" spokesman has a controversy placed at his lap, the very first question is the race of the people in question. Like any conscientious follower of Nazi racial policies, moral issues are always decided by racial factors. So when people like Farrakhan seriously speak of "white devils," his followers do not leave in disgust; they nod knowingly. Poor Lenin likes it that way. Divide us by race, and pretty soon we are lonely little atoms, like Winston Smith in *1984*, with nothing to cling to but the image of Big Brother.

Creating a "racially neutral" society and legal system, which was once the honorable goal of civil rights leaders, which included black and white people, has now been morphed into a racially focused society and legal system. Once, when black players were excluded from team sports, true opponents of racism denounced that and demanded the right of blacks to compete on an equal basis with whites.

Now, when about 13% of the American population is black, but 65% of the NFL players are black, we normal Americans who believe in achievement by merit, regardless of race, are not troubled at all. A disproportionately large number of great athletes are black. College and professional athletic competition, particularly in football and basketball, is highly competitive. Any program that discriminates based upon race will always be at the bottom of the league. But "civil rights" leaders are now complaining about discrimination against blacks in coaching. Although only 13% of the population is black, about 17% of the NFL coaches are black. So, although blacks are overrepresented in NFL coaching, this too, somehow, is white racism!

In the NBA, 83% of the players are black. At last count, 33% of the NBA head coaches are black. Almost one quarter of all NBA team presidents are black. If everyone viewed people only by their skin color, and not – as Dr. King so passionately urged us "by the content of their character" – then would an invidious pattern of discrimination against whites not be apparent? Not just whites – what about Hispanics? What about Americans of Oriental heritage? What about the dramatic under-representation of American Jews in professional team sports? Jews, Chinese, Hispanics, and others were certainly the victims of past discrimination, including admission to colleges where team sports were played. So why is there no push to have more Chinese players and coaches or more Jewish players and coaches?

The reason why is because, to everyone, it would look absurd. Races simply do not, and probably never will, break out into neatly calculated, statistically even numbers. No one with a mind and a heart feels that the NBA should have "racial quotas" or that black racism is the reason for black dominance in some areas of sport or music or entertainment. We should never judge a man by his color: that truth is common sense, but common sense is the enemy of Poor Lenin.

The little boy who cried 'Bigot!'

Bigotry is a real and ugly fact of human nature. There are people who dislike other people just because of their race, their language, their sex, their age or other factors which no one can control and which should not affect a person's judgment. We have laws against discrimination and we have a culture which looks down on bigotry (at least, most forms of bigotry.)

Unfortunately, though, instead of bigotry becoming something that just withers away, many people use bigotry as a crutch. They need to believe that racial or religious or gender or other prejudice runs as a deep undercurrent in American society because without a belief in bigotry lots of people would have to start treating ordinary people as ordinary people. So the tired list of insults - Racists! Sexist! Redneck! Anti-Semite! Homophobe! - have become almost obligatory in our society. Poor Lenin certainly accepts these accusations without much proof.

There is a danger to the little boy who cried "Bigot!" The overwhelming majority of Americans are tolerant. As one example, America is the first nation in the western world which had no real history of anti-Semitism. When nearly all Americans were devout Christians, Jews were accepted in all branches of government and society to a degree that stunned the western world. Women, although they suffered from some legal and political disabilities, were likewise treated as well in America as anywhere else on Earth. Blacks, Hispanics, Japanese, Chinese, Irish, Italians, and Germans were discriminated against, but – except for blacks – that did not last long or result in serious legal disabilities.

But there are a few people around who are truly anti-Semitic; there are a few white people who simply hate blacks (and blacks who simply hate whites); there are misogynists (and women who hate men, too.) The danger of assuming and accusing racism, sexism, and other forms of invidious discrimination as a general fact of life is that pretty quickly no one takes real bigotry seriously.

Poor Lenin, who sees an America of boorish crackers and brutal patriarchs, may believe that everyone of a particular race, sex, or religion is all bad, all bigoted, and all bullying. But of course that is not true. The reckless bigot-accuser may make some innocent people feel guilty, but hypersensitive reaction to imagined bigotry helps also to insure that no one takes real bigotry seriously. When even the mildest form of prejudice is treated like the worst excesses of a real racist like Bull Conner, then the really bad guys are thrown into the same vast hallway of the accused with jaywalkers and people who did not pay their library fines.

Wise Jews after the Holocaust correctly said this to their fellow Jews: Exaggerate nothing; the truth is more than enough to convict the guilty; be precise and truthful because pure and simple truth is our strongest ally. Eisenhower permitted any soldiers who wanted to tour the liberated camps to do so. No commentary was needed. No haranguing speeches were required. The truth, without help, carried the argument. If those who cry wolf had said that thirty million Jews died in the Shoah, he would have committed a great moral crime: Not a crime against the Nazis (who cares about them?) but a crime against the victims. Poor Lenin and his entourage love to cry "Bigot!" but when they do, it is the innocent they hurt and the guilty they help.

The mean shall inherit the Earth

Personal destruction, burning in effigy, murdering lives with savage ridicule - Poor Lenin taught all these tricks of his craft to Saul Alinksy. The rules he adopted were intended to be unfair. The rules created a system of terrorism as the means of ruling people. Saul might as well have been quoting Machiavelli, whose notion that the end justifies the means is blatant. People who follow The Great Faith, those of us who take the Ten Commandments, the Gospels, the notion of a Blessed Creator all seriously – whatever our specific theological beliefs – know that there is a Holy One, a Yahweh, a Father who knows, who cares, who records, and who rewards (or punishes) accordingly. We also know that each human being is special to this Lord.

The rules explained by Moses, by the Psalmists, by Jesus, and by St. Paul, insofar as a human behavior is concerned, are in accord. Murder is a sin. Stealing is a sin. Lying, destructively and maliciously, is a sin. Cheating on your spouse is a sin. Being jealous of other people is a sin. We are supposed to treat people the way we would like to be treated ourselves. Now what is crucial about these rules from the Infinite One is that these are not "bad tactics" or "unwise policies." These are sins. Criminal actions, lawsuits, and other interactions among humans may or may not come out of these, but sins against the Holy One are crimes against the law of God.

These laws are like laws of physics. Poor Lenin does not really believe in these laws at all. Just as the atheists of the French Revolution believed if enough eggs were broken, an omelet could be made, and just as Stalin believed that if enough Kulaks were killed the Soviet paradise would arrive, and just as Hitler thought that curing the world of the "bacillus" of Jews would make mankind healthier, Poor Lenin believes that these laws of the Almighty can be ignored. But His laws work perfectly: They grind slowly, but exceedingly fine.

This means that destroying enemies by any means – ridicule, threats, slander, deceptions, and so forth – never brings a better world. Contempt for the moral rules of the universe does produce a world with new, manmade standards replacing the standards of the Great Master of the Universe with a Brave New World in which the meek do not inherit the Earth, but rather the mean inherit the Earth. Whether they will want this Earth is a different question.

Picture Eastern Europe after the armies led by Poor Lenin's pupils, Stalin and Hitler, had fought over it for four years. It was no longer part of this planet but rather part of the netherworld. No moral person could hope that either side would win because the Mean had inherited this part of Earth. Murder, theft, rape, torture, arson, and every crime that the darkness of minds like Alinksy can conceive became reality.

Two systems on the "Eastern Front" held fast to the motto "The Mean Shall Inherit the Earth" and tested their tactics on each other. Abandoning the principles of the Great Faith produced human misery in lands which had once been happy, like the Baltic States. It did not matter much which pupil of Alinksy won that war – the little mustache or the big mustache – because victory itself, in the lands where they ruled, did not mean a return to a better world.

Those who believe "The Mean Shall Inherit the Earth" know what they want: they want the Holy One, with all His restraints on our behavior, to be banished, but more – they want the sentiment, the moral compass, the sweet smell of human kindness all crushed out of us. This does not mean that we should not embrace moral indignation – quite the contrary! It means that we must revile the very idea of right and wrong in methods. If anyone says that a tactic in pursuit of politically correct goals is a sin, then he must be destroyed as a…hypocrite. If anyone claims that envy is wrong, then he must also be made to feel the lash of amorality. As bad money drives out good money, so the deliberate policy of being mean infects everyone, even notional enemies. That is what Poor Lenin wants: the Mean Shall Inherit the Earth.

Ignorance of the law...is inevitable

"Ignorance of the law is no excuse" says the lawyer. But lawyers do not know what the law is half the time. Laws have force in society when laws are sensible, simple, modest, and direct. What we call "law" today is a pig's breakfast of federal statutes, federal regulations (often imposed by "regulatory" agencies simply given the power to make law), federal court decisions, state laws, state regulations, state court decisions, city ordinances...and so on.

Poor Lenin loves it that way. When laws and regulations touch everything in our lives and when these are hopelessly contradictory and incomprehensible, then the law loses all moral force. No one can know what the law is or even guess what the law ought to be. Our laws might as well be written in an ancient and lost language. When endless litigation, often lasting years, is necessary for judges and lawyers to "figure out" what a law or a regulation means, then how, in the world, are ordinary citizens supposed to know what they should or should not do?

In a society of laws, there are a few essential elements. The laws must be clear. People expected to obey the law must be able to understand the law. The laws must make sense. If the penalty for assault is greater than the penalty for murder, the law does not make sense. The laws also have to be something that a good person, someone who wants to do what is right, can intuitively understand.

None of that suits Poor Lenin at all. He does not want a society of law. He wants a society of chaos in which political muscle and self-interest determine what is "legal" in a particular situation and what is illegal. The ideal of good laws in the ancient world - the Ten Commandments or the Laws of Solon or the Twelve Tables of Rome or the Code of Hammurabi - offend Poor Lenin: these are too clear, too short, and too easily understood.

He much prefers a volume of federal regulations as big as a phone book full of minutia that no one can ever fully grasp. With that sort of legal system, everyone is innocent and everyone is guilty. The law, itself, means absolutely nothing. Everything depends upon who is held accountable to this so-called system of laws and how the legal cases are decided.

Poor Lenin also proposes laws as the "solution" to almost every problem. So Congress, the FDA, federal district courts, state legislatures, presidential executive orders, IRS regulations and a thousand other sources of "law" change what is legal and what is verboten as rapidly as water in a fast flowing river. Poor Lenin does not believe that the law should stay the same. The solution to problems in our society cannot be, say, people as free agents adapting their behavior. No: the solution must be new, changed instructions from the state.

IGNORANCE OF THE LAW...IS INEVITABLE

Even this process of making laws, Poor Lenin believes, must be murky. So when Congress passes a law, there are subcommittee hearings in both houses, committee hearings in both houses, a House version and a Senate version, a conference committee report and, of course, many bills so long that no mortal could read it all and no sane person would want to. Why is this complexity necessary? Well, if laws were made openly so that citizens could understand what was going on, surreal complexity would be fatal to enactment of the law. But if what Poor Lenin wants is a legislative process in which no one is really accountable, then the endless layers of unnecessary processes allows no one or everyone to be equally responsible for the new law.

Laws, once, were like the rules of football or baseball or basketball. Imagine a baseball game in which there were several sets of conflicting rules, and in which dozens of umpires issued written "opinions" of what the rules meant, and in which each year hundreds of new rules were adopted. Imagine a football season in which several important rules were modified halfway through the season. Would anyone doubt that this would hurt the game?

In those parts of life we take seriously, like professional sports, any rule change is a "Big Deal." There is extensive public debate before the actual rule change is considered by those empowered to make the change. Everyone knows precisely what the change will mean, and the rule change itself is seldom more than one new rule or a modification of a few words in the existing rule. This is because coaches, players, teams, fans, and sports analysts need and want to understand what is expected of them. The laws of football, baseball, and basketball are very hard to change.

Everyone understands that changing the rule on the strike zone, for example, utterly alters hitting percentages which go back one hundred years. Everyone knows that changing the types of tackles and blocks allowed fundamentally changes football. Even professional athletes who cannot read or write well understand the rules of the game very well — indeed, they would be very angry (and rightly so) if constantly changing complex rules were the real keys to winning the game.

Poor Lenin and nearly all his compatriots are lawyers. The real battles and conquests in life to them come not from fair competition in sports or efficiency in production or service in business. The real battles and conquests to them are all in courtrooms and legislative committee rooms. Because of that, ignorance of the law is... inevitable. The law is made, on purpose, impossible to understand.

If at first you don't deceive, lie, lie again

Poor Lenin does not have any problem with honesty, as long as it does not have any cost. He also has no problem with a world in which truth is "relative." Like all other totalitarians, Poor Lenin has no problem with presenting his spin on truth – the interpretation that helps him acquire and hold the only thing that matter to him: power.

Hitler had his "Big Lie." Stalin proclaimed that any lie which helped the revolution was fine. Mussolini said that invention was better than truth. Poor Lenin and his companions do not believe that lying is wrong. President Clinton under oath responded famously to a question by asking "It depends upon what your definition of 'is' is." John Kerry remembered serving under President Nixon in Christmas 1968 while in Cambodia – only none of his boat mates (even the few who liked him) recall being in Cambodia and it is historical fact that Nixon was not president in 1968. Al Gore invented the Internet (and, apparently, using a time machine to go back several decades to do it.) John Edwards looked right into television cameras and lied about having an affair, even as his wife was sick with cancer.

It is not that Poor Lenin or Slick Willie or their friends are the only people who lie (almost everyone in life lies at one time or the other.) It is rather that Poor Lenin and his compatriots have no qualms about lying. They lie without blinking an eye. They fib without a single neuron in their brain out of place. They lie for the same reason that they bribe friends with tax dollars or pretend to be bipartisan when legislation is cooked up far in advance of any involvement of their partisan rivals. They lie because there is nothing in their life which separates truth from lie. Their minds do not think in terms of honesty and dishonesty. Their minds think, instead, in terms of spin and effect.

Ideology is truth to Poor Lenin. So any questions or problems for which he might want a real answer are simply punched like an old computer into the Orwellian misology which Poor Lenin believes, word for word, with vastly deeper intensity than, say, a Moslem suicide bomber believes in the Koran. The ideological answer is always true and questioning the ideologically correct answer with tiny things like facts or history is beneath Poor Lenin.

The ideology itself is painted up with various colors and decorated so that sometimes it is called "socialism" or "feminism" or "environmentalism" or "liberation theology" or "progressivism" but those words, also, mean nothing. Feminists, for example, are utterly indifferent to the welfare of women and socialists have no interest in the misery of the poor. The quilting of odd, misshapen patches into some grotesquerie passing as a system of thought is the biggest lie of all. Just as the Nazis were utterly indifferent to the welfare of the German people and the Soviets were utterly indifferent to the welfare of the Russian people and the Maoists were utterly indifferent to the welfare of the Chinese people, so Poor Lenin and his pals are utterly indifferent to anything they pretend to care about. They – surprise! – lie about this indifference. What do they care about? Look at the only thing they really seek: power.

In the beginning, Darwin created the Heavens and the Earth

The divine origin of the universe and life reflects the thinking of humans since earliest history. The universe is not an accident. Our planet was formed following physical laws, but there was much more than just physics and time involved. Life is not the product of lightning bolts in primordial mush creating proteins which over a few billion years became cells of life and which then evolved through natural selection into human consciousness.

Life, especially human life with consciousness of its own mortality and its ability to use words to capture information over time, was willed by a Creator. Great scientists like the late Sir Fred Hoyle have worked out the impossibility of evolution through natural selection on Earth. No scientist, even if natural selection could have worked, can explain how the universe itself began.

Whether we wish it to be or not, human beings are extraordinary creatures whose very existence proclaims the reality of God. But no Sinisterist dare acknowledge that. Sinisterists must be gods and they must be the only gods. What transcends them also transcends their feeble knowledge, their fleeting lives, and their corruptible motives. So God, Yahweh, Allah, Ahura Mazda, every name for the Holy One who made us all must be intellectually destroyed.

Darwin (and others) proposed theories of how life could diverge from a single replicating organism into the whole panorama of life we know today. These innocents, (as any genuinely honest atheist is an innocent), did not intend to father Marx and his children Mussolini, Lenin, Hitler, and Poor Lenin. But that is just what Darwin did.

Lenin understood just what a liberating myth natural selection could be. If nature was god, then men – at least certain men – could be gods too. So Kulaks, Jews, Poles, anyway, really, who did not fit into some men's pseudo-divine plan for mankind could be disposed of without concern. Poor Lenin and his companions could tell any lie, inflict any horror, defile any tradition, and commit any crime – if it only helped the "party" to create Heaven, which was, of course, a manmade Heaven on Earth.

This Heaven, even if it could be made, is doomed by the same raw forces of nature which, supposedly, made planets, stars, and life. The Bolsheviks and Nazis could war, murder, enslave, deceive, torture and corrupt for a hundred years and even if they made their "heaven" after that, a stray asteroid or a returning, ancient comet could utterly destroy it all in the blink of an eye.

If we know that Darwin is not God or God's prophet, then we must, somehow, construct our lives around a universe built with some end in mind. Moral rules matter then. If we cannot make ourselves into immortal gods, and if we may someday face the One who made us, then how we live matters much more than the scraps of science we can farm on Earth.

The Tanach has words which answers Lenin's proverb and these words read "In the beginning, God created the Heavens and the Earth." The deeper truth, if we are not the blessed creatures of a Blessed Creator is this: "Vanity of vanities," says the preacher, "vanity of vanities. All is vanity." Everything ultimately, but God, is a vanity. Even Darwin.

Charity begins at (someone else's) home

Charity is a virtue deeply engrained in Judeo-Christian values. There are few civilizations which have not viewed charity as good and important. The proverb "Charity begins at home," however, declares that before helping other people, those who live in your home must have enough food, clothing, and shelter. Parents owe more to their children than to the children of others. This is a far cry from saying that we have no duty of charity to hungry children around the world: of course we do. And if we are fat and they are skeletons, then we are being selfish and mocking our duty of charity.

The greatest help that each home can give to the world is to support itself. Organized charities, even personal charity, cannot replace parents and children working for the good of their home. Dependence upon charity is, in a fashion, a type of enslavement. There are times in which this is necessary. Natural disasters, wars, diseases, economic crises – all of these can throw the willing wage earner onto the sickbed of charitable dependence.

When that charity comes from a friend, a family member, a church or synagogue, then those receiving charity want to end that dependence as soon as they can. Only the psychologically maimed think depending on friends for food is good. When the charity comes from the welfare worker acting as an agent of the state, then the value of charity is even more demeaning.

In that case, charity does not begin at home (as it should.) It does not begin through any voluntary giving at all. Charity, in fact, is not charity at all. It is simply the involuntary taking of property from some and giving it to others. When "charity" – really government vote buying – begins in some political clique, then everyone is degraded.

The dependent subject is urged to remain dependent (so that the bureaucrat will still have his job and the legislators supporting the program will have their bought votes.) Those bureaucrats and politicians are degraded by becoming, effectively, fences of stolen property. The producer is robbed and then he is condemned for complaining about the robbery.

Charity begins, but emphatically does not end, at home. Also, all charity is volitional or it is not charity at all. Religions enjoin the rich to give, and God backs that duty up with His caution as well, but even in religions like Islam, which provide that the giving of alms to the poor is one of a few very serious moral duties, does not command that alms be given to the "Bureau of Alms Collection and Distribution."

Organized charity, even coerced support for the poor, is sometimes necessary in modest amounts and in special situations. But only in Poor Lenin's Almanac do we find

CHARITY BEGINS AT (SOMEONE ELSE'S) HOME

a proverb which requires the collection of taxes, the payment of party officials (or whatever bureaucrats may be called), and the distribution of a survival stipend to dependent clients.

Thou shall not commit monogamy

Traditional marriage is under attack by Poor Lenin. Radical Islam accepts the notion of polygamy as a part of Islamic law, and Osama bin Ladin has multiple wives. The Soviet Union made divorce easy, almost ridiculously easy, because it was a bourgeois convention, a relic of "Capitalism." The Nazis had breeding farms, in which German maidens were impregnated by virile Nazi studs: marriage, monogamy, and fidelity to anything beyond the needs of the party were not given the slightest thought.

The modern "progressive" speaks of how silly to think that a man and a woman should marry and stay married for life. It is so…unnatural. In a sense, it is: people are not really animals, the way that "progressives" think of animals, and so, unlike all but a few species of creatures, people "marry" rather than simply procreate by hopping from filly to filly. The sexual revolution was a revolution which took us out of the human realm of morals and sin and brought us instead into the inhuman realm of amoral beasts and androids.

What is it about the traditional marriage which so bothers some people? It provides a structure for children of both sexes to grow up with respected roles in human society. These families give an added, nongovernmental safety net: not just two parents who can work, but two sets of grandparents who could help (if those families also stayed together), and aunts and uncles who could help. Think of just how many social problems are "solved" by a Jewish or Christian married couple who have been happily married for thirty years? What is the welfare rate for this demographic group? (I suspect, in thermodynamic terms, it is around zero degrees Kelvin.)

The traditional, stable, permanent family is the worst nightmare of anyone who would like to run your life. When life is home, family, children, neighbors and friends then it is almost as bad for our would-be gods as if people went to shul or to church regularly and believed in a Blessed Creator. The family provides a meaning for life, a security in life, an emotional commitment to life which allows people to be perfectly happy without throwing blood on women in fur coats, handing out needles to drug addicts, worshipping at druid woodland shrines or other purposeless motions invented to consume the tedium of an empty existence.

Traditional families produce traditional grandparents, who are infinitely better equipped to help children with problems than hordes of disinterested, salaried social workers. The child welfare industry depends heavily upon dysfunctional families. Sociology professors require that children need more than parents, grandparents, and a good home. Self-anointed "advocates" for children need to have shattered homes in the same way that junkies need to have heroin. No, this does not mean that all these professions consciously want bad marriages, multiple divorces, and other familial debris. But it does mean that they thrive when traditional families falter and that they face famine when people marry, have kids, and stay happily married for life.

So, Poor Lenin must enjoin his disciples against this threat: "Thou shalt not commit monogamy." Untraditional marriages? Serial polygamy – many marriages? Children out of wedlock? All of those promote problems, in one way or the other. Monogamy, lifelong marital commitment, these require personal commitment as well and that, very likely, relies upon religious commitment as well. All of this leads to happy, self-reliant people who just produce happier, self-reliant people (and so on.) This is a wholesome condition that Poor Lenin forbids.

I never met a bureaucrat I didn't like

Will Rogers, the delightfully wise commentator on the human condition, loved people. He did not see people as black or white, male or female, gay or straight, Christian or Jew, Okie or New Yorker. He saw people the way God intended us to see people: as creatures with souls, consciences, hearts, mothers, fathers, dreams, and fears. Will Rogers saw people as people.

Poor Lenin does not do that. People, broadly speaking, fall into two categories: state or party officials, on the one hand, and those ruled by state or party officials, on the other hand. The bane of our age is bureaucracy. It gobbles up initiative, ideas, and innovations and crushes them into long, dull, deadening reams of official regulations, policies, laws, and rules. Bureaucrats inhabit bureaucracies. They guard whatever the orthodoxy happens to be at the moment. Bureaucrats are mortal enemies of the free market, whether that market is an economic market, an educational market, a philosophical market, or any of the other myriad market of human interaction.

Poor Lenin, when he ran the old Soviet Union, loved bureaucrats. They ran the Soviet Empire…right into the ground. These bureaucrats are not just government officials – thinking so is a mistake – many Soviet bureaucrats, just like many Nazi bureaucrats, worked for the party or some association or organization created to advance goals which almost always look noble on paper.

In America, these bureaucrats sit in big corporations as well as government offices. Every regulation dealing with affirmative action, job safety, medical leave, environmental protection, labor relations or any other aspect of government management of private businesses requires not just a federal bureaucrat, and a state and city bureaucrat, but also a corporate bureaucrat working with these government bureaucrats and making sure that each of them has plenty of paper to push back and forth. These bureaucrats also lounge around law firms and courthouses, foundations and universities. Anywhere that orthodoxy needs to be imposed, a bureaucrat is there. All of these have profoundly vested interests in keeping anything from changing, but creating the illusion of activity and thought.

This is just what Poor Lenin wants. If policies and decisions conform to reality, then how can Poor Lenin create reality? That's no fun. There's no profit in it either. Policies and decisions must always flow from above, from men who would be god. Bureaucrats are the paid army of these rulers. They do not deliberately try to do harm. Often, they fancy that they do good. But the fact is these bureaucrats are like those German generals who said after the last great war "I was just following orders."

I NEVER MET A BUREAUCRAT I DIDN'T LIKE

Poor Lenin loves that attitude. Personal conscience, religious morality - stuff like that - are - an obstacle to Poor Lenin's dream of dystopia. That is why he never met a bureaucrat he didn't like. We should not be individuals, thinking for ourselves. We should be cogs in the machine – government, party, institution – the difference among various forms of bureaucracies does not matter much to Poor Lenin. Poor Lenin, like his dear friends Hitler, Mussolini, and Mao, wants every single one of us to be a bureaucrat of sorts: busy – ever so busy! – doing something for the movement or the cause which is, on reflection, really nothing.

People who visited Nazi Party headquarters in Munich before the war were flabbergasted by the huge numbers of bureaucrats who had, literally, nothing to do but to make work for other bureaucrats or for hapless businessmen and other productive people trying to keep up with the ocean of bureaucratic paper. Poor Lenin would have found Munich Party Headquarters doing just what it should be doing – shuffling reports no one reads and issues orders that make no sense, all by hard working Nazi Party bureaucrats.

One picture is worth a thousand lies

Poor Lenin loves images. People connect to images emotionally. People react to images. Information technology once confined mankind to the dreary limitations of text – just books with words, and maybe a few illustrations. Clear, written words are poison ivy to Poor Lenin. As Winston Smith in *1984* could have told you, a written record is a thoughtcrime. How can Poor Lenin keep rewriting history, so that the past conforms to this moment of Poor Lenin's propaganda, if these books keep telling a different story?

Sure, Poor Lenin produces books, but as vehicles for propagating the faith (in Poor Lenin), books can be embarrassing. Imagine Poor Lenin seeing someone reading a book published in 1940 which vilified Churchill and his resistance to Hitler, spoke gently about the Nazis, and blamed the "capitalism" of Britain and America for the Second World War! Now imagine the same author in 1942 wrote a book calling the war against Hitler as democracy's fight against aggression! Only Orwell could make sense of the two books, and for that reason old books are very dangerous to Poor Lenin.

But text itself is very dangerous to Poor Lenin. As Bradbury described in *Fahrenheit 451*, books can cause a variety of very serious social problems: individuality, reflection, expression, permanence, definition, cognition, independence, and countless other diseases of liberty. One book – one really good book, like Torah, the King James Bible, *1984*, *The Road to Serfdom*, or *The Gulag Archipelago*–can ruin a perfectly safe regime.

What of the books that Poor Lenin publishes? *Das Kapital*, like *Mein Kampf*, were bought in large numbers in those particular provinces of Poor Lenin's power in which an ornament was needed on the bookshelf, but who really read these long, rambling books? Who read, The *Myth of the Twentieth Century*, Nazi theorist Alfred Rosenberg's *opus minus*? Which delusional Soviet citizen actually read *Izvestia* or *Pravda* and expected anything beyond the dreariest cant?

No – what Poor Lenin needs are images. He needs Hitler addressing an audience at night with lights turning the night sky into an exciting dark vista. He needs pictures of Poor Lenin everywhere ("Big Brother is Watching") and everywhere the image is the same: benign, wise, omniscient, strong. He needs films, television programs, and music in America which tell us that those who believe in God are mean-looking bigots, that those who love America are narrow-minded super-patriots, and that those who live in stable homes are neurotic deceivers.

Poor Lenin needs images of Bill Clinton looking kind and friendly. He needs the voice of Barack Obama to be soothing and calm, just as his appearance is invariably smart and young. Poor Lenin needs film cameras to capture, then carefully edit, just what he thinks is best for the people to see and hear (and by seeing and hearing, ultimately, to believe.)

A photograph of Whitaker Chambers as an overweight, sweaty, and physically unattractive man is precisely what Poor Lenin wants. A photograph of Alger Hiss as a cool, handsome, popular man is precisely what Poor Lenin wants. Even today, when the guilt of Alger Hiss is beyond the range of any honest, sane mind to doubt, the images of Alger Hiss (or Judith Coplon, long presumed an innocent victim of virulent anti-Communism, and now undoubtedly pure traitor) are worth a thousand words.

Poor Lenin does not want us thinking: he wants us feeling, and he wants us feeling just exactly what suits his purposes, which always boil down to getting him a power fix. The more we think, the less power Poor Lenin can have. The more we use pictures, not words; the more we rely on images, not reason; the more power Poor Lenin has.

An abortion a day keeps the babies away

Poor Lenin is very (overtly) solicitous of the welfare of children. If a physician discovers that a child has obvious problems, like depression or drug abuse, he has a legal and moral duty to report it. Doctors also have been surrounded with the barbed wired of litigation if they perform any sort of medical procedure without the full, informed consent of the patient, the patient's parents (if she is a minor), and perhaps even Aunt Tillie.

But Poor Lenin loves nothing so much as ending the beating heart of a little baby in the womb. When that malicious contempt for life is combined with the tender fears of a young girl in trouble, then the pleasure of slaughter by Poor Lenin is unbounded. What more could one ask of life (or, rather, death) than killing the unborn child of a terrified pregnant child? How about making money from the crime?

Normally Poor Lenin eschews the profit motive, but when the destruction of innocent life is involved, he thinks that proper financial motivation is fine. No government regulation can inhibit this process either. The government may regulate whether you have a pond or not on your land. It may boss people around when it comes to the type of light bulbs in their home. There is almost nothing which is outside the proper purview of the busybodies of government.

Except when it comes to the extermination of "viable fetal mass" everything must be unregulated. And this holy rite of fetal homicide is enshrined in the Constitution. It is far too sacred to leave this sacrament to, say, Congress or state legislatures. These assemblies, which are no more that the duly elected representatives of the people, lack the property authority to require that baby slayers in the medical profession provide psychological counseling before performing their deed, or that they must meet special standards of care, or that they must insure that at least the young girl tied on the rock before the altar of Baal understands just what is being taken from her.

A baby without a contract out on it is given great deference by Poor Lenin. Mothers should be careful what they eat, what they drink, what they smoke, what they do. Prenatal care, aside from execution of the baby, is very serious business. Sonograms, precious pictures of the baby moving, the little one sucking his thumb, the evidence of sentience – these are all very special things – if a baby is no on the hit list.

Outside the womb, in the room, the baby is the object of infinite care and attention. Do not smoke around a baby – this is strictly Verboten! Poor Lenin wants to begin state supervised care for this potential voter almost as soon as it can begin to sense the world around it. Preschool should begin at, say, ten months and continue until Kindergarten, which will lead to school, which will lead to college – and so forth.

Poor Lenin also seems to view pregnancies as "accidents." The notion that God brings a soul into the world when a man and a woman create an unborn human seems preposterous to Poor Lenin. Life itself, to Poor Lenin, is an accident. No purpose, human or divine, can lurk behind the creation of human life – or so says Poor Lenin. Even primitive savages knew more than Poor Lenin about the conception of human life. This bringing of human life from human life is a holy thing, whatever one's religion. That "viable fetal mass" will one day grow up and look you straight in the eye. The man or woman who was once a fetus will love, think, pray, weep, hope, strive, beget, and die.

How odd – how truly and utterly odd – that Poor Lenin could think that an acorn or an apple seed which grows into a tree is sacred, but that a baby, the seed of mankind, is not. But that is just what Poor Lenin thinks, and babies are burdens to many people. Thus Poor Lenin preaches: an abortion a day keeps the babies away.

I pledge indifference to the flag

Poor Lenin, like so many others before him, loves to live in America. He loves to live in America even more than he loves to loath America. He emphatically denies that he is unpatriotic, but very few people ever accuse him of being patriotic. The blood of slain patriots who gave their lives so that he might live in freedom bores him. George Washington? How passé! Douglass MacArthur? An American Mandarin! George Patton? A quasi-fascist nutcase!

Poor Lenin thinks nothing, in time of war, of calling one of our greatest generals, "General Betrayus" or revealing secrets of how we are winning the war on the front pages of the *New York Times* or accusing our soldiers (without proof) of razing villages and raping virgins. No accusation is too outlandish, no defamation too extreme, no conspiracy too nutty when it comes to attacking the United States of Amerika.

Yet Poor Lenin will not leave America. He will complain openly and loudly about living in a fascist state (a form of protest which he could never do in a fascist state), but he will never, ever leave to dwell in a land that suits his values better. Instead, Poor Lenin says, America "needs" his moral instruction. He wants to "change" America into something better. The world is threatened by America, Poor Lenin proclaims, and so he is actually doing a service to everyone by staying in America and trying to turn it into something that more resembles the rest of the world.

In fact, Poor Lenin is just another wife beater. Poor Lenin mopes around the house, telling everyone how crummy his wife is, how lucky she is to have him, and how helpful it is to her for him to slap her around every once in awhile. She – his wife, America - is the problem, not him. If she wants a divorce – if America prefers not to live in the same house with some creep who always complains and regularly abuses her – then she, America, is the problem – certainly not Poor Lenin!

Poor Lenin stays in a home he professes to despise because (Poor Lenin claims) he owes it to the world to get America into shape, to correct every petty fault that he can find in her, to try to destroy her happiness, to malign her appearance and manners, to mock her accomplishments, to take money from her purse and then to come home drunk and vicious.

The idea that Poor Lenin should leave a homeland which he claims makes him so miserable and angry, the notion that it is in everyone's interest for him to leave a home which he claims causes him to rage so violently, never seems to cross the mind of Poor Lenin. It never occurs to him that when millions all around the world try to get into America at almost any cost and when tens of millions have left their homes in other lands, traveled across the oceans, and made a new home here that maybe they know better than Poor Lenin.

Endless ships of Italians, Jews, Irish, Poles, Vietnamese, Koreans, Germans, Greeks, Swedes and other immigrant peoples were just ships of fools. Poor Lenin understands, if they do not, that being born a citizen of the United States is not a blessing but a curse. If hardworking people from Mexico come into America with their families at great risk and labor, then they, too, must just not get it.

If men and women who escaped Nazi Germany or Stalinist Russia or Maoist China get teary eyed when they consider the promise of America, well what do these people know? Poor Lenin just considers America, like any abusive husband considers his wife, as the "old ball and chain," the cause of his own unhappiness, and never, ever, deserving of any real respect. If there are people from all over the world who proudly pledge allegiance to the flag of the United States, Poor Lenin yawns very publicly. He pledges indifference to the flag.

They shall make unto thyself many idols

What, exactly, is an "idol"? Well, it is the token or image of a false god. The proverb lifted from the Ten Commandments which warns men against worshipping things that are not God is precisely wrong to Poor Lenin. The fact is that the world was created so that man could live in it – that is what Judeo-Christian teachings say - and a thousand progressive preachers and Reform rabbis cannot change that. The things on Earth or the things which, with our imagination, we can invent or conceive of from Creation are not divine. If we worship them as if they had meaning greater than God, or even greater than us, then we sin – something Poor Lenin wants us to do.

The good things in life – health, beauty, intelligence, education, prosperity – are just that: good "things." Often the good things in life are the result of dumb chance. Someone born in America during the last century began life much better off than someone born in North Korea or Somalia. People are born rich or poor, and while they can affect that during their life by effort or by sloth, the starting line is pretty important. Beauty and intelligence are, to a very large degree, a matter of heredity. There are people with naturally strong and healthy constitutions and people with naturally weak and sickly constitutions.

We each, to a large degree, can affect our position in life through hard work and serious study, but chance often has a lot to do with where we are in life. Accidents, too, have much to do with it. An athlete or a beauty queen can, after a car wreck, be changed forever. In the end, no matter what we do or how well we do it, we die. This is the first important truth we learn from life: it ends.

There is a part of us, however, which is not subject to accidents or fate. It does not ever die. Fate does not cheat us out of this part, because it is beyond the power of mere Fate: it is in the hands of God. Our soul, our conscience, our heart, our good or bad works – this part of us matters. The man who does as much good as he can, given his mean station in life, is vastly better than the disinterested, billionaire philanthropist.

We live in an age in which it seems that we can do almost anything – but really, we can do almost nothing. All the technology, all the medical miracles, all the information available at the blink of an eye – all of those things are simply representations of an idol. Poor Lenin does not grasp this (or does not want to grasp this.) He looks at poverty, and sees the sum of human problems. He looks at ignorance, and sees the hope of every problem in our thinking. He looks at health, and sees the answer to all our social problems.

Health, education, welfare (and self-esteem, intellect, appearance, and other worldly virtues) do not merit worship. When we worship them, we worship false idols. We cannot make Heaven on Earth. That is precisely what the Nazis tried to do. They were very health conscious, eschewing tobacco and alcohol, endorsing exercise and pre-natal care. They loved nature. They had high self-esteem. They had very sophisticated technology. They might, ghastly as it rightly seems to us, have succeeded in "breeding" a race of men who were smarter than the rest of us. They might have wiped out hereditary diseases.

So what? What they did was ghastly in the eyes of the Almighty. That, and ultimately that, alone, matters. There is nothing wrong with being health conscious, working hard to be affluent, exercising your mind, learning all you can, taking care of your appearance, and so on. In fact, in proper doses, these are evidences of a joyful and earnest soul. But when we begin to see health itself as a deity to be worshipped, when we imagine that education actually cures moral sicknesses, or when we fancy that self-esteem alone makes us better, we are worshipping false gods.

The irony, which Poor Lenin has never understood, is that if we place the Blessed Creator first and if we recognize Him as the only thing in the universe worth worshipping, then as a consequence of that (because He loves us), many of the "good things in life" come along in the wake of that worship. When we fall down before false gods like Health, Education, and Welfare, then we often lose even those objects of worship and we end up sick, ignorant, and poor.

In judges we trust

When a society rejects the idea of a Blessed Creator, as Poor Lenin insists that we must, there is a void which can only be filled by an authority greater than man. Monarchies which have a hereditary ruler work fairly well: everyone knows that the King is only the King because of an accident of birth. He does not claim any special authority beyond that. Generally monarchies have devolved over time into limited, constitutional systems in which the King is a neutral mediator. His authority comes, specifically, from being perceived as neutral and above the fray.

Poor Lenin finds this highly unsatisfactory. He wants people to replace God, not simply rule by the grace of God, and those people need to be the sort of people who are viewed as having special powers and insights. Judges fit that role perfectly. Although the law is simply the creature of men, the manufacture of citizens, Judges can become witch doctors who divine its hidden meanings and purposes. So a reading of the United States Constitution can "find" a shade of an totally unmentioned right of privacy and then can intuit that this imagined right of privacy extends to the body of a pregnant woman. Voila! Judges have done what mortals could not: the Constitution, apparently, has granted women a right to prenatal infanticide.

Scour the Federalist Papers or any other source material from the time of constitutional debates and there is no mention of abortion at all, although the practice is old.

Congress, in the Constitution, is granted only a few enumerated powers. But Judges, supposedly protecting us from the excesses of government, magically find that the very limited powers of the federal government are, in fact, infinite. Because a meteorite falling from the sky could, theoretically, "affect interstate commerce," Congress has the power to regulate the heavens. Judges "interpreting" such an absurd reading of the Constitution nod solemnly and agree that Congress can do, basically, anything.

Judges have determined that a black man in America can never be a real legal person (in *Dred Scott*), and that public accommodations which are "separate but equal" do not violate the Equal Protection Clause of the Fourteenth Amendment (*Plessy v. Ferguson*), and then later can routinely uphold invidiously unequal treatment of white people or men as a "remedy" for past wrongs: "The Judge Giveth. The Judge Taketh Away. Blessed is the Name of the Judge."

Poor Lenin does not really believe in law, which is what makes the rule of judges so wonderful to him. Because judges can take plain text and, through legalistic alchemy, transform black into white and white into black, law – always a preserve of rights against abuse – can be turned, instead, into a weapon against the people.

It does not matter that Poor Lenin can find in American history almost no example in which judges actually led the way for reform. (For example, the Supreme Court, for decades after the Civil War, was the principal obstacle to Republican Party efforts in Congress to free the black man.) It does not matter that when real danger has lurked, like in the deportation of Japanese-Americans to internment camps during World War II, judges did nothing to end this wrong. It does not matter that the "interpretation" of constitutional rights of the accused in criminal cases during the 1960s produced – and was predicted at the time as certain to produce – a dramatic increase in the rate of violent crime. It does not matter that forced school busing did incalculable harm to millions of children, wasted vast amounts of fossil fuels, polluted the environment, and interfered with family life and education for no purpose at all.

What happens is the judges give Poor Lenin the equivalent in America of the Politburo in the old Soviet Union. Unaccountable, unaffected by the horrors of its meddling, unelected by anyone, judges can be little gods and do whatever they fancy. If removing God from any mention in public life is part of that mischief, fine: judges wish no other gods before them.

A penny earned is a penny taxed

How long does the average taxpayer work to pay his tax burden? Poor Lenin believes, of course, that no one has any right to anything that does not pass first through the halls of government. But because people are used to supporting themselves, the utter elimination of private property is not (yet, at least) possible.

But government can tax…and tax…and tax again. The Supreme Court, in one of its rare lucid moments, once stated "The power to tax is the power to destroy." That would suggest that unless we wish to give government the power to destroy our lives and our liberties, taxation must be limited. In theory, Poor Lenin wants to tax the productive (it is not really "the rich" who are taxed; it is the income-earners – the producers.) In practice, Poor Lenin wants to tax as a way of keeping people helpless.

If the average producer works half of his year just to pay Poor Lenin's bureaucrats and party hacks, then the producer can be kept in check as easily as the Medieval lord kept his serfs in check. The life of the producer, then, is largely the property of Poor Lenin. That is what matters to Poor Lenin. He wants power. He wants control.

Common sense would suggest that over time, as private productivity increases, the need for government to tax us would shrink, not grow. Affluent Americans need very little from government, really, except for protection and elementary systems of commerce, which could even be user funded like turnpikes. The more money the middle class has to spend, the easier it is for the poor to enter the middle class. The modest and necessary government functions require only a small percentage of the average tax burden, and the richer our nation the smaller a percentage of national income is needed for these necessary functions.

But Poor Lenin would tax the rich into the middle class and the middle class into poverty even if the tax dollars collected were all burnt as sacrifices to some odd deity. It is not the fact that the government needs money which drives our tax systems. It is, rather, the fact that the government (when run by Poor Lenin) needs us not to have money. That is why half of our working life is spent on the feudal fiefdoms and the vast plantations of Poor Lenin. He needs us never to get too independent, never too financially secure, and never too affluent. So, despite the fact that our needs have never been less, the rate of taxation – not just the amount of revenue taxed! – keeps growing. A penny earned is a penny taxed.

An ounce of celebrity is worth
a pound of merit

Poor Lenin understands that people no longer really pay attention to anything except the fleeting moment of now. People (Poor Lenin is no exception), like to be seen, to be heard, to be noticed. It does not much matter anymore how one is noticed. Friends of Poor Lenin are always getting arrested for using drugs, driving drunk, bearing children out of wedlock, and otherwise outraging public decency. As long as people are talking about them, nothing else matters.

Everyone wants to be a "rock star," even though by most accounts many rock stars live in a self-created Hell. Everyone wants to win elections and "serve" in Washington, although the reek of Washingtonian moral sewage makes much of the air of America almost unbearable. Everyone wants to write a "tell all" book, although these books are not exactly the same sort of book as the Confessions of St. Augustine.

No sentence for any crime is worse, at least to Poor Lenin, than a life sentence of working hard each day at a meaningful job, coming home to a quiet neighborhood of family and friends, communally thanking the Blessed Creator for creating a blessed world, and enjoying the simple pleasures of life. No: men and women like Poor

Lenin need more than an ordinary and honorable life. It might be hacking your ex-wife to death a few decades after your fame as a great football player has faded. It might be dumping buckets of blood on middle class women wearing fur coats in the winter. It must, however, be something which makes people notice you.

If you are the president, perhaps it means making a "major policy statement" every other day. If you are a congressperson, it may mean treating businessmen like criminals, to the hoots of appreciative audiences. If you are an "expert" (and who isn't?) it may mean finding the long suppressed cure for a barely noticed affliction.

In this world of celebrity, every human problem is a "social problem" and every "social problem" requires "education, awareness, and collaboration" – and especially a lot of attention. Private responsibility - going into your home and quietly praying to the Almighty for strength, hugging your spouse and asking for help, sitting quietly and thinking about your life - these all lack the PR factor. Who – I mean, besides Your Maker, your spouse, and yourself – are going to know about all these valiant efforts?

So Poor Lenin and his flock find in celebrity the sort of immortality, the sort of meaning, and the sort of spiritual immersion that God, family, and courage can never hope to provide (at least, to Poor Lenin.) If Poor Lenin's friends only dimly notice that as the price of "attention" grows higher and higher, as the market demand grows more intense, as more and more people just want to be noticed, that just doing good and being honorable has become so blasé as to be worthless, then that dim awareness changes nothing.

Real craziness, true irrationality, not just destructiveness but self-destructiveness, more and more are the price of celebrity. But that's okay. Poor Lenin lives in a world inhabited by corrupt politicians, drugged sports stars, vain and brainless starlets, and mavens of nihilism. The maturity level is just below the five year old on the driving board yelling down "Mommy, watch me!" If there is no water in the swimming pool, no mater: an ounce of celebrity is worth a pound of merit.

Tyranny is in the eye of the beholder

Who was Mao Tse Tung? Was he an agrarian reformer who ended the thuggish rule of the Kuomintang? What about Fidel Castro? Was he a guerilla fighter who threw out a Right-Wing dictator? Outside of our own nation, where Poor Lenin sees a fascist around every corner, Poor Lenin sees the world full of misunderstood leaders who happen to hate America.

Fidel Castro seized power in Cuba fifty years ago. At the time Castro seized power in Cuba, the island had the second highest standard of living in the Western hemisphere. Health care was better in Cuba in 1959 than it was in France or Italy. There were huge numbers of opposition newspapers and many radio and television sets with many radio and television programs. Cuba was not a purely functioning democracy, but it was hardly a nonfunctioning democracy.

Before Castro, the Cuban people were not getting on leaky boats and trying to float to Florida. In fact, immigration into Cuba was as common as emigration out of Cuba. Were there political prisoners in Cuba before Castro? A few, but not prisoners kept for decades in horrific prisons. Batista had actually won free, fair, and open elections to earn his first term in office. He was rather like

Peron in Argentina – a populist ruler who wanted to soak the rich and who pretended, as much as he could, to chart the "middle path" between Communism and Capitalism.

When Castro drove him out and seized power, all the flunky reporters and editors who listen to every word of Poor Lenin suddenly found out that Batista was a "Right-Wing Dictator." This doubtless came as a surprise to the Cuban Communist Party, whose members had served in his cabinet and who had long supported Batista. It must also have flabbergasted American diplomats in Cuba, who had been warning Washington that Batista probably was a communist.

Fidel must have really been to the Left to make Batista look like a "Right-Wing Dictator," right? Well, not exactly. Fidel devoured the works of Benito Mussolini. He consciously modeled his speaking after Adolph Hitler. When Franco died, Fidel declared a national day of mourning. What made Castro so popular with Poor Lenin?

Well, in the Second World War, Batista was the strongest Latin American ally of the democracies war against Germany and Italy. When Peron was toying with the Nazis, Batista was opposing them (as well as Falangist, Fascist, and Japanese agents in Cuba.) Batista opposed Hitler even when the party line of Poor Lenin required opposing Churchill in his battle with Hitler. Batista, in short, did not follow the party line.

Poor Lenin and his successors tried to extend the reach of their empire as far as possible but the infuriatingly pro-American socialist, Batista, remained on the best possible terms of America. Batista's policies enriched the lives of the Cuban people but, of course, the welfare of the Cuban people - in the poker games of Poor Lenin - is the Deuce of Clubs. So the anti-Fascist socialist leader of Cuba was processed through the Ministry of Truth and, magically, became a Right- Wing dictator, while the proto-fascist Fidel, because he hated America, became thrilling, charismatic, magnificent, etc., ad nauseum.

Poor Lenin also still views the greatest mass murderer in human history, Mao Tse Tung, as an "agrarian reformer." Mao essentially sat out the Second World War, while Chaing and his Party of the People provided resistance to Japanese forces without which Asia would have fallen to Japan. Still, Poor Lenin thinks it was good for Mao to overthrow Chaing. Mao took a Chinese nation which had been accepted as a major ally and represented at conferences before the end of the war, and he turned China into closed society frozen for decades out of world contact. Still, Poor Lenin thinks it was good for Mao to overthrow Chaing. Mao provided indispensable help to North Korea which not only allowed that ghastly realm to survive, but to grow into a nuclear power that starves millions of its own people to death. Mao began in 1949, the very year he took power, the genocide of the Tibetan people, a real crime which infuriates American Leftists (who never grasp that this horror began because Chaing, who did not war on Tibet, had been driven from power.) Still, Poor Lenin thinks it was good for Mao to overthrow Chaing.

Why then did so many followers of Poor Lenin find Mao so appealing? He believed, really, in nothing – not even Marxism. He was the ultimate "Man God" in the world. He loathed America; he loathed religious faith; he loathed any party operatives who showed a hint of humanity or independence.

Were Batista and Chaing angels? No. They were, in modest ways, lukewarm dictators. But they really tried to succeed in improving the lives of the people of their islands, Cuba and Taiwan, and they succeeded. They sought friendship with America. They did not scorn and punish Judeo-Christian traditions. They were surely imperfect, but incomparably better than ghoulish characters like Castro and Mao. So why does Poor Lenin find those latter two leaders so much better than the former two? Because, as in all things, the motto of Poor Lenin is "The worse, the better" (and it does not get much worse than Castro or Mao.)

Our Father, who art in Washington

America was not founded in Washington D.C. In fact, when the new American nation was declared in 1776, there was no Washington D.C. When the first American government, the Articles of Confederation, was created, there was no Washington D.C. When the Constitution was written, there was no Washington D.C. When the Constitution was ratified, there was no Washington D.C. When George Washington was sworn in as our first president, there was no Washington D.C. It was not until The Organic Act of 1801, after Washington had left office as president, that the District of Columbia was formally a federal polity.

Since then, it seems, this once harmless bit of real estate has worked like a black hole that swallows up all the power, prestige and influence in America. There was nothing particularly ennobling about the District of Columbia. The location of the federal district – in Maryland and next to Virginia – was part of a compromise to placate slave states by placing the home of the federal government between two slave states. The Potomac River is notoriously unhealthy in the summer and not too pleasant most of the year.

Because of its location, the British were able to despoil our capital in the War of 1812. Because of its location, the

Army of Northern Virginia under Robert E. Lee fought needlessly bloody battles in Virginia and Maryland in the American Civil War. Because of its vast distance from the American West, during our westward expansion honest frontiersmen needed to rely upon lobbyists and other unsavory types for help in building railroads and making internal improvements.

Washington D.C. was established as our capital after our Revolutionary War, whose Declaration of Independence complained of the great remoteness and inconvenience of London to the colonials. Washington D.C. is actually farther from most of America than Philadelphia is from London. Washington D.C. is a political crime waiting to happen. Or, rather, it is a repeat political offender.

Wholesome proposals like term limits would be much less important if the federal government was located, say, in Wichita or Little Rock. But Poor Lenin loves Washington D.C. After the Bolshevik Revolution, the new Tsars of Russia tried to pretend that all the peoples who had been trapped in the Russian Empire – Estonians, Ukrainians, Armenians, and the rest – were now "free." What happened instead was that the power of Moscow grew even greater than even before. The Soviet Empire was more centralized, not less centralized, than Tsarist Russia.

When the Nazis took power in Germany, the very first dramatic political change was to destroy the power of the states. Under the Weimar Republic and under the Imperial German system, Bavaria and other states of Germany were largely sovereign powers. But the Nazis ended the power of German states as an initial step toward enslaving all Germans. The destruction of the rights of states or provinces or grand duchies (in the case of Tsarist Russia) was one of the best signs that Poor Lenin was crushing every center of power which could resist the Kremlin.

America, to Poor Lenin's great sadness, vests vast powers in sovereign states. He has the same low opinion of Canadian provinces, Australian states, Swiss cantons, and the old United Provinces of the Netherlands. Robust and independent state governments with real power to resist the central government almost always lead to such troublesome issues as individual freedom, resistance to commands from the party, limits on the otherwise unlimited power of government, and so forth.

Seizing as much power from state government and placing as much power in Washington, D.C. is exactly what Poor Lenin wants. Poor Lenin needs a plan to run our lives. He does not need or want any real power to reside with state assemblymen or governors, each with a different vision of America tailored to the values and culture of a particular region of America. To paraphrase one of Poor Lenin's favorite pupils, a nation like America (or Germany) cannot tolerate regional power and local diversity. Instead, Poor Lenin and Hitler require "Ein Volk! Ein Reich! Ein Fuhrer!"

Thou shall covet everything
that is thy neighbors

Anyone born in America is lucky. Anyone who has enough to eat is lucky. Throughout human history, political liberty and enough food were luxuries for the nobility, in most cases. But Poor Lenin cannot stand satisfied people. He certainly cannot stand people who are grateful. So he invents the myth that those who do not have everything that they want must be deprived because others, unfairly, have more than they deserve.

If you build a whole system of thought around the sin of envy, it is called "socialism" or "communism." Perhaps this noxious theory had some vague seriousness in past ages, when the poor were hungry and when life was short and dangerous. But modern America is full of "poor" people whose biggest health problem is obesity. What is the greatest emotional problem of most Americans? It is boredom. What is the obsession that screams at every woman at every grocery checkout counter in America? Beauty – however that is defined – and the lifelong struggle to look as beautiful as you can, even though we all age, gray, and wrinkle as we pass through our life.

Coveting shifts responsibility for a life from the person actually living that life and onto those who are perceived to have better lives. It demands utter equality, even if utter equality means equal misery. Everyone in life is differently situated. No one is better off in every way than anyone else. Hollywood starlets end up as drug addicts – why? Football stars go to prison – why? Even those naturally blessed with gifts that, on the surface, are far greater than most of us often end up in tragic circumstances.

Coveting also means that it is easier not to sympathize with our neighbor. If he has something we want, human nature (or its bad side) can trick us into thinking that what he has is really important to him. It may or it may not be. He may want what we have. We can only guess what is in someone else's heart and mind. The rich man may be rich because he has given us years of his life in work, in study, in risk, and in tears. But if we want his wealth, then we do not want to see that.

We may have frolicked while he struggled. We prefer not to know that. Poor Lenin helps us with that. He removes us from self-examination by focusing attention on the good things that our neighbor has, not the difficulties he has overcome in getting those good things. The more we blind ourselves to the true price of what we want, the more we deceive ourselves into believing that taking without asking is some sort of "fairness."

Life is not fair, though. It is not fair in any sense of the word. The wisest man lacks the wisdom or to grasp even the tiniest portions of someone else's burdens in life. We have the power to do good, but when we fancy that we have the power to implement cosmic justice, we cross the fatal line of toying with sin into living a life of sin. Doing good, loving mercy, being just — these are universal rules of human behavior which do not fail in the long run.

If we want true, pure, living justice in our lives, the only option is an Almighty who can be just, and who alone can grasp every nuance and motive, every bit of luck or tragedy, and every earned or unearned thing. Turning to men for real justice means unleashing the demons of our envy and our jealousies and turning those demons to greater demons of men like Hitler and like, of course, Poor Lenin.

.

Have Yourself a Merry Little Ramadan

No malice so delights Poor Lenin than the slander of Judeo-Christian theology in general and Christianity in particular. So when pseudo-Christians like Jeremiah Wright pretend that asking God to Damn America is some bizarre form of Christianity, Poor Lenin is more than willing to believe that. Wright is about as Christian as Bishop Muller, the Reichbishop in Nazi Germany appointed by the Nazi government to promote their anti-Christian religion called "Positive Christianity." What did that mean? It meant a "Christianity" in which Jesus was not Jewish, the Old Testament was ripped out of the Bible, the New Testament was ripped out of the Bible: no Gospels, no "Rabbi Paul," as these pseudo-Christian Nazis called him, no Sermon on the Mount, no Golden Rule…but aside from that!

The slightest acknowledgement of the God of Jews and Christians in the public square must be ruthlessly suppressed. It does not matter that most of the original American states had established state churches (not just separation of church and state, but actually particular branches of Christianity that were state religions) – and yet these very states were often the most tolerant of all religions. It does not matter that the most open nations in Europe like England, Norway, Denmark, Scotland, and Sweden also had specific established state churches. The grand myth that somehow Judeo-Christian faith, the primary spiritual source for the world's acceptance of tolerance, is intolerant persists.

The same is not true of Islam. Many Moslems are peaceful and condemnation of an entire religious group is unwarranted. But the demand that Islam, a minority religion in America and a religion contrary to the principles upon which our nation was founded, should be granted a special place in our culture while a crèche in the city park is strictly verboten is not proof that we have become more tolerant. It is rather proof that those who are truly intolerant, like Poor Lenin, who cannot apologize enough for the putative sins of this superficially adopted faith, want one specific system of belief to fail and want another, Islam, to succeed.

Islam was viewed very early on by the Soviets as something less a religion and more a political movement – and a political movement of the global proletariat. Nazis, the other grand socialist system of the last century, also loved Islam almost as much as they loathed Judaism and Christianity. Mussolini, who was an atheist in practice, was proud to be called "Defender of Islam." There is no problem with Iranian students, many of whom I worked with, simultaneously believing Stalin and Hitler were good men and considering themselves devout Moslems.

HAVE YOURSELF A MERRY LITTLE RAMADAN

Poor Lenin and his friends would celebrate Ramadan just like they would celebrate Earth Day or Kwanza or May Day in Moscow. They will be happy to put in the public square, into the elementary school, on PBS or NPR, in any publicly supported forum at all, anything that celebrates the faith of the intolerant ones – radical Islam, Nazism, Marxism, radical environmentalism, Fascism and the like. But that other religion, the one of devout Jews and Christians, must be scrubbed clean from every part of the people's government.

Those who can, do. Those who can't, sue

There are no accidents in God's universe. So, at least, goes the thinking of Poor Lenin, (except that Poor Lenin never thinks of it in terms of a Blessed Creator.) He does, however, think a lot about secular sin (also known as legal liability.) People unable to succeed in life are often victims of circumstances. Someone who wants, for example, to be an NBA star is a victim of circumstance if he is less than six feet tall. A guy who wants to win the Miss America Pageant is also a victim of circumstance. Someone born into a lower middle class home is probably not going to take the Grand Tour of Europe. Someone from North Dakota is going to have a tough time being a world champion surfer.

Bad things in life happen to everyone. Death, in fact, happens to everyone. Sickness and injury happen to almost everyone. Practically all of us lose loved ones. We apply for jobs that we do not get. We create art and writing that no one seems to want. It is the easiest thing in the world to blame others for our misfortunes. Sometimes that is true. Polish Jews in the Second World War, for example, were almost completely victims of circumstance. Children born with serious health problems are in the same boat. Natural disasters create horrible pain and loss, without anyone really being at fault.

But Poor Lenin finds someone blaming others is the best tonic for any hurt in life. This is fairly easy to do on a broad scale in which all individuality is squashed (and Poor Lenin loves nothing more than a soul mashed into mush by a monstrous social machine), but it is harder to do when misfortune befalls someone with no official, sanctioned, certified, victimhood.

What if, for example, Kentucky Fried Chicken served a chicken breast which was too crispy and a white Baptist male dentist chokes to death? Poor Lenin believes that such a tragic accident is also an opportunity to do mischief. Kentucky Fried Chicken is a rich corporation. A good trial lawyer, who can find fault in Heaven, will see some culpability on the part of the rich corporation. Although the lawyer could not fix a broken tooth or, for that matter, cook up a good fried chicken dinner, he can convince judges and juries that Kentucky Fried Chicken must be to blame.

The proliferation of litigation means that another variation of that most blessed creature in Poor Lenin's world, the bureaucrat, gets to grab some power. Not only does the dentist's wife get a hunk of dough, but so does the lawyer's essentially parasitic partners and staff — but that is not all! Kentucky Fried Chicken will need to hire bureaucrats to check quality control, so that no one ever dies at a KFC restaurant again. State and city inspectors will doubtless need bigger budgets and more staff to help protect us from the dire menace of an extra crispy chicken breast.

THOSE WHO CAN, DO. THOSE WHO CAN'T, SUE

None of these folks, of course, is actually "doing" anything useful. They are not providing a good or a service that someone wants. They are not cutting your grass or canning your food or defending our nation from enemies or patrolling our streets or putting out fires or watching sick patients. But then, "Those who can, do. Those who can't, sue."

The perfect is the friend of the bad

No one is perfect. If you seek to find fault in anyone, you can. This means that anyone who maintains that moral standards exist must also maintain that we all fail to meet those standards. Albert Schweitzer and Mother Teresa, doubtless, had moments of human failing and moments of weakness in the face of temptation. Poor Lenin finds this fact of the human condition a very convenient truth. "None of us are saints!" he sneers. Well, yes, some of us are saints and some of us are monsters.

The existence of imperfection in the human condition is not, as Poor Lenin wishes for us to believe, proof that we are all morally about the same. Churchill had moments of weakness and could blow up at his staff. Hitler was kind to animals and had moments of pleasing charm to women. So what? We are not judged by minute, isolated, and discrete events. We are judged by the sum of our life.

Poor Lenin, who believes that sin is a myth and that evil is just opinion, loves to turn his principles (or rather, his emphatic rejection of any principles) against his enemies (good people.) Sometimes this is very hard work. Ronald Reagan, for example, was such a palpably decent man that Poor Lenin was forced to invent his moral failings. That surely does not bother Poor Lenin, but it makes it much harder to convince his motley disciples.

When Sarah Palin's daughter was pregnant before marriage, this somehow "proved" that Sarah was a sinner. Sarah Palin, of course, never would deny that she was a sinner – she would insist that all of us are sinners – but the idea that a common moral failing by her daughter is equivalent, somehow, with Hollywood starlets promiscuously having children out of wedlock and proclaiming that this is fine is an absurd conclusion.

Poor Lenin finds "good" in everyone, and indeed, there is good in everyone. But pretending that a single tender impulse of Stalin or Hitler is equivalent to a lifetime of noble deeds by John Paul II or Billy Graham is obscene. What Poor Lenin wants, of course, is the end of moral standards, the end of moral judgments, and the end of morality itself. He finds Torah and the Gospels repellant, and the only truly bad people in the world to Poor Lenin are those who think that anything can be bad. It does not matter that scriptures provide perspective to sin. It does not matter that a Jew, during the High Holy Days, can make amends appropriate to his sins and proceed into a new year clean. It does not matter that a Christian can confess his sins to God, and if he is sincere in a desire to sin no more, can be washed of the sins. Poor Lenin finds this the height of hypocrisy.

So any peccadillo of anyone who believes that moral standards exist must be displayed for every eye and every ear in the world. While the most grotesque crimes of the moral evil men must be somehow "understood" in the light of circumstances, upbringing, viewpoint, and so forth. Because some good people sin and because some bad people do good deeds, in rare moments, no one is good and no one is bad.

This is essential to Poor Lenin, because Poor Lenin lives by the motto that the end justifies the mean (or the meanness.) One can't make an omelet without breaking eggs! Believe that, and pretty soon Poor Lenin's acolytes spend an inordinate amount of time making omelets instead of other types of dishes. Trying to live a righteous life, to Poor Lenin, means being that worst sort of person…a hypocrite. He does not accept the belief of normal, decent people that hypocrisy is half sin and half virtue: a person preaches what is wrong, but does not always practice what he preaches. Instead the sin of the hypocrite, to Poor Lenin, is preaching that anything is wrong.

Either a borrower or a spender be

Poor Lenin has "virtues" which are not virtues at all. He depends upon the rest of us living in ways that are certain to keep us dependent. Poor Lenin wants our government to behave that way and to encourage us to behave that way as well. So the old maxim, from Shakespeare's Polonius "Neither a borrower nor a lender be," is turned on its head by Poor Lenin: "Either a borrower or a lender be."

If the American economy is collapsing, what should we do to make it better? (Let's put aside, for the moment, that the last thing that Poor Lenin wants is for the economy or anything else to actually get better.) Well, why not borrow an enormous amount of money from the federal government which can, after all, just print more money any time it wants. Then spend the money. Spend it on almost anything. If you want full employment, for example, why not pay people to walk down the street throwing trash on the road and then pay other people to follow them around picking it up? Why not hire people to watch daytime television programs at home, and then fill out dozens of government online forms to prove that they, indeed, watched the shows (that would also require creating a new Bureau of Television Watching Workers Auditing.)

Once Poor Lenin persuades us to abandon the idea that wealth comes from productivity and that productivity comes from efficiency and that efficiency is simply a variant form of thrift, almost anything can be done in the name of helping people. Recall that Poor Lenin's icon, FDR, paid farmers to plow under crops while much of America and the world went hungry. Productivity and efficiency come from all those little businesses which go around creating meaningful jobs and real wealth.

Poor Lenin sees no reason to do this, when it is so much easier just to borrow money – it can always be paid back at inflated interest rates – and then to do just what Dale Carnegie advised: Win Friends and Influence People. The piper never needs to be paid, apparently. So, although the national debt per person in 2009 was $37,000 or $168,000 for a family of four, who cares?

And so what if, at current rates, the national debt will soon exceed our nation's GDP (Gross Domestic Product)? Can't we just borrow more to pay that debt? Or raise the tax rate to a reasonable level, like, say, sixty percent? Or perhaps when we literally owe more than we produce in an entire year, we can just enter a rather absolute period of austerity. These are all questions for policy wonks.

Poor Lenin has figured out that raising taxes raises ire. This is not because raising taxes on the "rich" is unpopular. The propaganda that those who earn a million dollars a year hardly pay any taxes is still a solid urban legend. The problem is that the milk cow is dry. If Poor Lenin confiscated all the wealth of "rich," it would barely dent the national debt.

As a consequence, the only way to raise revenue by taxation is to raise taxes on the middle class and the poor. Ouch! They might well notice if their take home pay suddenly dropped about twenty-percent in one month. They might even stop believing that Poor Lenin was trying to help them build a better society through endless borrowing, wasteful spending, and taxes which only really come from the top one quarter of the income earners.

So, let the debt grow! Let federal dollars, and lots of other forms of manure, help the flower gardens grow! Let every program ever conceived be tried as evidence of our compassion. Let us leave our children with heavy iron manacles which keep them enslaved forever (Hey, at least they should thank us that we didn't abort them!)

To err is human, to forgive ideological

Perfection is the enemy of the good, we all know, but Poor Lenin believes that only perfect matters. A good nation is an imperfect nation. A good person is an imperfect person. A good people are an imperfect people. Poor Lenin, in accord with the writings of that sage, Saul Alinksy, hater of Heaven and enemy of morality, knows that the easiest way to end morality is to make it an impossible standard (for those who maintain that moral standards exist) and to deny that any moral standards exist for followers of Poor Lenin.

Life, of course, is full of mistakes and many of these are moral mistakes. The Judeo-Christian tradition fully endorses the idea that true repentance is what the Blessed Creator wants and that all of us sin, so all of us, while trying not to sin, should not be afraid to admit our sins. This process of redemption also involves the recognition that truth and honesty really exist.

Poor Lenin does not believe in the existence of real truth any more than he believes in the virtue of honesty. So he never has to admit any moral shortcomings at all. He and his comrades (an apt term!) simply deny ever doing anything which is unethical, dishonest, or otherwise immoral. When confronted with manifest immorality, the vice is explained as a misunderstanding or a misinterpretation or another viewpoint or anything other than a confession of sin.

Poor Lenin also fully grasps that, unlike him, his enemies – good and decent people – do believe in goodness and decency. They have a sense of shame. When they fail to live up to their standards, they understand what is required of them. In a society of normal people, this is healthy and natural. Washing hands and body with soap and water makes a fellow clean. On the other hand, people like Poor Lenin believe that filth is simply a matter of opinion. There is no need, ever, to admit that one's heart and soul have been sullied.

So Poor Lenin and his buddies can present themselves to the world as angels or at least unflawed humans. He can hold those who feel the weight of sin up to the gallows and the pillory, making the case that they are hopelessly flawed because they are somewhat flawed. The slightest sin is mortal, in the anti-theology of Poor Lenin.

Anyone who believes adultery is wrong and whoever commits adultery is beyond redemption… the other option is to stop believing that adultery is a sin. Anyone who has ever gotten drunk faces the same verdict: guilty of a capital crime or innocent. Standards of behavior which are not the whim of man and judgments which are based upon broad patterns of a life and true repentance for mistakes do not count to Poor Lenin.

TO ERR IS HUMAN, TO FORGIVE IDEOLOGICAL

What counts to Poor Lenin is not real morality but political morality: Who is following the party line? Who is doing what Poor Lenin has declared "fashionable"? Who is advancing "the cause"? Who is helping Poor Lenin gain and hold power? Those are the sorts of people who, in Poor Lenin's thinking, are morally right. When people fall in life, when we make mistakes of different sorts, as we all do, the only question for Poor Lenin is who is acting ideologically properly. Being politically correct is the only form of confession which can redeem anyone from his sins. To err is human, to forgive is ideological.

Do Mr Jew? I expect you to die

Goldfinger, in the James Bond movie of the same name, answers Agent 007 with famous words, as a laser is about to bisect the secret agent. In response to a question by Bond asking Goldfinger what James Bond expects him to do, Goldfinger responds: "Do, Mr. Bond? I expect you to die." This is just what many Arabs and Moslems want the Jews in Israel to do. Think about it: the Jewish people, who, almost alone in the last two thousand years, have had no home, have asked for a Jewish homeland in Israel.

The land is not valuable. It is not large. It does not sit astride oceans of oil, like Saudi Arabia or Kuwait. It does not have vast hordes of gold and diamonds, like South Africa. Rubber, which once was great wealth, built opera houses deep in the Amazon, but rubber does not grow in Israel. Cotton once drove much of the global economy and built mansions in the South, but there are no plantations in Israel.

Some nations sit astride vital points on the globe. The island of Singapore guards the Straits of Malacca; the Rock of Gibraltar overlooks the western approach to the Mediterranean; the Dardanelles and Bosporus were the keys to Trojan power and wealth; San Francisco Bay is a huge harbor which grants riches with little work; Panama has a canal that holds cuts marine travel time in half. Israel, which has nearly always been a battlefield of greater empires, once held half of another great canal, Suez, but the Jewish people gave their half of that canal away for just the hope of future peace.

The people of Israel have tried to do all they can to show their peaceful intentions towards the huge populations and lands which surround them. As the only free, affluent, democratic nation in the regime (after the vivisection of Christian Lebanon by Islamic extremists), Israel had much to offer those people who chant angrily for justice in the mobs of Arab and Islamic cities. America has worked and bled to create oases of ordered liberty in Iraq and in Afghanistan, and its efforts, like the efforts of Israel, have met with universal contempt among those who live to hate.

But America, at least, can withdraw. Israel cannot. Israel does not deny non-Jews the right to vote. In fact, Arabs are members of the Knesset. It does not fill its government press with anti-Islamic counterparts of the Protocols of the Learned Elders of Zion. In fact, many of the most passionate defenders of Arab and Islamic rights in Israel are professors – state employees – of universities.

What does the world expect of Israel? What do the Arabs and the Moslem extremists expect of Israel? If a Jewish homeland could be created by doing what the Dutch did and creating polders from the Mediterranean

Sea, does anyone doubt that this new land reclaimed by Jewish engineers from the sea would not, magically, become "Palestinian" land?

In fact, if Jewish engineers reclaimed polders in the Red Sea and Mediterranean Sea, created hundreds of square miles of fertile farmland, and constructed comfortable towns and villages throughout these reclaimed lands – and then gave the lands to the Palestinians – does anyone really think that this would "solve" the Palestinian "problem" or that a single Palestinian or a single Arab government or a single Moslem government would commend the Israeli government for this gesture of goodwill?

No, of course not! Poor Lenin knows this, at some level anyway, and he simply does not care. The Arab world is poor because Israel is affluent. The success in life of any group of people is proof of their malicious exploitation of others. It does not matter that Libya, Iran, Iraq and other Islamic nations sit on one of the greatest windfall profits in history – vast reserves of easily recovered oil – while Israel sits on…a narrow strip of relatively arid land. Israel must be punished for the crime of proving that the Arabs could do much, much better if they worked as well as they hated. But Poor Lenin understands their "case." So when Arabs talk of reclaiming Palestine (by ending Israel), Poor Lenin just yawns.

From little ACORN mighty trees vote

Poor Lenin maintains that everyone in a democracy has a duty to vote. Why? Well, because we need to balance the serious, thoughtful, informed, and ethical voters with the comical, silly, ignorant, and bribed voters – I guess. It has always been something of a mystery why voter participation levels are so important to people like Poor Lenin. In the old Soviet Union, of course, nearly everyone voted – whether they wanted to or not. Turnout in Nazi Germany and Fascist Italy was also very high. Because, it seems, Poor Lenin draws great inspiration from these totalitarian regimes, maybe he feels that sending truckloads of voters to polling booths legitimizes his own policies.

Actually, if no one felt very motivated to vote, it would indicate an incredibly healthy polity: people would, by their indifference, show how content they were with the way things were being run. When people cannot wait to vote, it indicates that our nation is badly divided, that many people are unhappy with government, and that elections – rather than simply being some of the choices in a well-lived life – have become the center of everything.

If someone went to the doctor once a week, we would either think him very ill or very neurotic. An annual checkup is about all that more sensible people want out of their doctor, and if someone could tell them that seeing their doctor only once every couple of years was fine, that would be good too. But Poor Lenin thinks that simmering rage and obsessive interest in elections is evidence of a healthy nation.

Elections are so important, in fact, that nothing can be left to chance. Poor Lenin knows well Chicago, where elections were far too important to be left to the voters. Political campaigns are part of Poor Lenin's life, like the "Bread and Circuses" of ancient Rome. Let people rant and rave, bicker and contend. Just don't let them actually elect their leaders.

From little ACORN, mighty trees vote. The way to win elections is to cheat. Register Mickey Mouse and Elmer Fudd (or, perhaps, Charles Manson and the Boston Strangler.) "Vote early and often" as the old maxim of Chicago politics goes. Throw away honest ballots of our opponents and replace them with imaginary voters who vote for the slate of Poor Lenin.

If someone protests that Mickey Mouse should not be allowed to vote, then claim "voter intimidation" (after all, Mickey for far too long was denied the right to vote!) A true democracy must include more than simply mature citizens. It must include illegal aliens, grade school children, household pets, convicted felons, and fictional characters. Once 18 year olds could not vote, as if the age of the voter mattered at all! Soon ACORN will be insisting that children in first grade vote, that the vote be done in the class, that the right vote cast be part of the student's grade, and that the NEA appointed vote counters report the results.

Soon, ACORN hopes, the number of votes cast in elections will actually exceed the population of the nation. What a triumph for democracy that would be! There is a caveat, though, about who can vote. Dogs, cats, inmates in prisons or insane asylums, terrorists awaiting deportation, and the like – all these should be allowed to vote in any election. Preschool children should be allowed to vote too (preferably during a commercial on Cartoon Network), but only children of a certain minimum age can vote.

So while a babe in swaddling clothes can vote, a babe alive and moving in his mothers womb has no right to vote at all. In fact, ACORN would never grant any rights at all to "viable fetal mass." The very seed of human life, the very acorn from which the mighty oak will grow, is, in the minds of Poor Lenin and his ACORN vote collectors, nothing at all. Not even equal to Mickey Mouse.

All the news that's fit to hide

The *New York Times* has a motto which once, perhaps, reflected a real policy: All the news that's fit to print. This meant to reflect that the media in America would report the facts, editorialize (give its institutional opinion), and then allow its audience to form their own opinions. The best thing that a good newspaper editor or reporter could do was to get a "scoop" – a story that had been missed by competing newspapers. It was hard to fill up a newspaper, especially a daily newspaper in a big city. So the more stuff you could find out, the more different bits of information that a reporter could uncover, the better.

That did not mean newspapers were unbiased. In fact, many newspapers were openly partisan: the word "Democrat" or "Republican" was in their masthead. So, if you were a Democrat in one big city and you wanted to get all the news, but hear your side of the story, you would buy one newspaper. If you were a Republican, you would buy another newspaper. People who took current events seriously would typically buy three or four newspapers and read them all.

Woe to the newspaper that ignored a big story just because the story did not fit into its ideological universe. Very few people read those newspapers. The sheer amount of information in a daily newspaper was so enormous that ignoring a big story was dangerously gross incompetence: Who, in the world, would want to fork out good money for a newspaper that kept the reader ignorant? Maybe a periodical could be pure bias in Stalinist Russia or Nazi Germany, but not in America.

But Poor Lenin and his friends really do not need to know what happens in the world (ideology will dictate current events and trump facts), and he certainly has no interest in people actually getting all the information about what is happening in the community, the state, the nation, or the world. So the media, the cronies of Poor Lenin and his pals, simply decide what is "news" and what is not "news." If Poor Lenin takes his wife to the theater in a new suit, that is news. If a scientist produces compelling evidence of global cooling, that is not news. If Poor Lenin decides to give yet another speech about his latest idea for making Heaven on Earth, that is news. If his critics uncover very shady business dealings by Poor Lenin and his pals, that is officially "not newsworthy" (or, if it must be printed, it is treated as newspaper filler, the inside column of page 34.)

The contents of news stories themselves are carefully edited. So, a congressman who sexually molests a sheep is a "Republican" if he is a Republican, but he is a "Congressman" if he is a Democrat. If he supports cutting taxes, he is an "arch-conservative," but if he opposes cutting taxes, he is a "moderate." Periodicals like the *New York Times* and the broadcast counterparts like MSNBC are companies that, if their product was pharmaceutical, would be sanctioned by the Food and Drug Administration. Their "news" is simply snake oil. The broadcasts and the newspaper pages are so filled with vast amounts of blather, tired theories pretending to be new facts, and bias once reserved for commentary sections or editorial pages, that one could read and listen to them all day and never really learn anything. So much of the real world does not fit into their ideological reality, that most of the real world is simply hidden. This, Poor Lenin's friends consider, all the news that's fit to hide.

What's good for the goose is not good for the gander

The Violence Against Women Act was enacted to protect geese (women) from violence. The idea that the gander might also be the victim of violence in a relationship was simply unthinkable. Women are good. Men are bad. That has been the mantra of feminism for many years. Odd then that men, who alone had the vote for so long and who, presumably, held all the other cards (money, physical power, legal rights) voted to give women - who were disenfranchised, terrorized by men, lacking legal protections, unable to acquire money like men – the right to vote. Yes, women protested – a few, anyway – but the only thing that women could really do was to appeal to the consciences of men.

The contrast between the Women's Liberation Movement and other movements is profound. A bloody civil war and decades of subsequent terrorism and Jim Crow laws kept blacks oppressed, and appeals to conscience did not really work very well. The right of the working man to organize in strikes was often surrounded by great violence, terrorism, and hardship.

The Women's Liberation Movement revealed, by the very passivity of its opposition, that quite obviously women were never oppressed at all. Rich girls, educated at Vassar, screamed at construction workers and garbage collectors how oppressed women were in America. Most women, like most men, just worked hard and tried to get through life as best they could. The lucky ones found a good man or a good woman to share their life, to buy a home, and to raise a family.

What was good for the goose was different for the gander. To the great shock of Poor Lenin and every other Leftist, women and men turned out to be fundamentally different (these ideologues are people, obviously, who have never done any hard work on a farm.) So…the fact that men naturally performed certain types of work in society and that women naturally performed other kinds of work in society was not the result of a vast masculine conspiracy – well, you could have knocked Poor Lenin over with a feather!

Even more amazingly, these roles for men and for women tended to be pretty much the same roles all over the world. In cultures and in civilizations that had almost nothing else in common, the sexual roles were very similar. The puzzle got even more puzzling: these roles also tended to correspond to the physical, mental, and emotional differences between men and women. This did not mean – and men never believed (except for a few male equivalents of "feminists") – that men were better than women or women were better than men. It meant, instead, that they were different in many ways.

Even more amazingly, the differences between men and women in human society tended to correspond to the differences between males and females in higher animal life. Male lions had prides of females, and the adult male always ate the kill first. Although there was not a perfect symmetry, the general pattern over the spectrum of higher animals was quite clear. Was nature, too, part of this vast masculine conspiracy?

But feminists prevailed in the policy arena. Those powerless, disenfranchised, discriminated, impoverished women succeeded – oh, somehow! – in creating a huge bundle of programs (all supported enthusiastically by Poor Lenin) to help women…and none to help men. The Violence Against Women Act specifically prevented any help being provided to protect males. So, its funds could not be used for programs to help an abused baby boy be removed from the custody of his abusive mother, but it could be used to make the case that the nonviolent father should not be given the child.

Quotas, affirmative action, and all the rest made some sense, perhaps, in the case of blacks and other minorities who suffered from discrimination. But women? Most of the wealth in America is owned by women. Most of the votes in elections are cast by women. The life expectancy of women is greater than men. The most dangerous jobs (the sort that in Mississippi once would have been designated for blacks or in India for "untouchables" or in Nazi occupied Europe by Jews and by Poles) are done by men, not women.

The vast majority of women understand that they are, in no sense of the word, truly victims of society, particularly American society. Women are favored in some ways, disfavored in a few ways, and treated the same in most ways. The different treatment nearly always is based upon natural differences between men and women. The overwhelming majority of convicts in prison are male. Who thinks affirmative action in that area would be fair or good? Black "leaders" rail that the disproportionate number of blacks in prison means that the criminal justice system is stacked against men, so doesn't that mean that the disproportionate number of men in prison mean that the criminal justice system is stacked against men?

The result is that Poor Lenin and his ladies' auxiliary propound the preposterous tale that government programs and laws should be changed to give more rights and more goodies to women. What is good for the goose is not good for the gander. The goose and the gander are very different. Society, not government, can best sort out of the differences. Nature has been doing that for a long time quite well.

Low self-esteem goeth before a fall

Poor Lenin thinks that high self esteem is, probably, the most important part of any life. None of us, after all, are sinners. The very idea of sin is one of the worst things man has invented! It caused George Washington to do stupid things like admit to his father that he cut down a cherry tree (what good could come of that?) We should all be proud – really proud! – of who we are. So we squander the blessing of being born healthy in America? So we treat the love of God for us like it was a candy bar? So what?

The important thing in life is to be proud of just who you are. Only if you feel good about yourself can you be truly happy. High self-esteem has been the source of so much joy in human history. The Nazis, for example, had very high self-esteem, and look at all the good they did! The Emperor Caligula thought himself not only a god, but the greatest of the gods, and did anyone question that? – Nooooo! Jim Jones at "Jonestown" had self-esteem coming out the ying-yang, and he was an excellent motivator. Does anyone doubt that Kim Jong Il or Fidel Castro also have very healthy levels of self esteem?

Now consider all the problems of low self-esteem. George Washington could have become the King of America or he could have been re-elected forever as president, but instead he served two lousy terms and left us with all the messiness of self-government. Abe Lincoln was always humanizing himself with self-deprecating humor – and he got murdered! Ronald Reagan did the same thing (always joking about his age, falling asleep in cabinet meetings, and that sort of stuff) and yet Poor Lenin only bows to the false image of Reagan, not to the real man.

What we really need are prostitutes, pimps, pushers, and pornographers who are really proud of their work. We need do-nothings who revel in their uselessness. We need people who understand that merely breathing merits accolades. Kids don't need to "honor" their parents. Unwed mothers need feel no disgrace in their "choice," any more than mothers who decide to murder the babies in their wombs need to be gloomy or ashamed.

After all, there is no right or wrong – except for the wrongness of feeling constrained by honor, by principles, by duty or any of that other silly stuff. If we all just realized how great we are (and by "we," of course, I mean "you" and "I" – because the rest of the world is just full of losers), then most of our mental health problems would just fade away.

If we just knew that there was no reason for us to try hard at anything – work, conscience, prayer (oh, God!), honesty, patriotism, or any of those other bothersome elements of "character"- then we would be as happy as chimps in a banana tree. Low self-esteem is the cause of nearly all my problems. I know, because I know darn near everything. If you don't believe that, just ask me.

Parents should be seen and not heard

Poor Lenin cannot understand why parents take such an interest in the moral and social development of their own children. The role of the sperm donor, egg donor, and incubator is pretty much finished after birth. At that point, the vital process of proper socialization becomes the job of the state. What on earth could parents know about parenting?

Poor Lenin understands that the deconstruction of family values and the reconstruction of the resulting mess of scattered parts into a suitable worker ant (or drone, as the needs of the hive may require) requires as little interference with parents as possible. Parents, of course, vote and they are sensitive folk (considering that they, not Poor Lenin, are responsible for their offspring.)

So Poor Lenin creates the impression – the grand impression! – of parental involvement by having parents seen in schools, at meetings, and so forth. Poor Lenin even helps instruct the parents what their jobs are in raising their own children (much of it, like school work itself, is simply "busy work.") It is vitally important that Poor Lenin show parents, really concerned parents, in a lot of settings around the institutions he, not parents, really run.

But the actual thoughts, wishes, and opinions of parents are another matter entirely. They have not had the years of training, the semesters of political indoctrination, necessary to inculcate liberal thinking (i.e. hard line Leftism) into the minds of children. Parents might, carelessly, lead children to think, to question, to explore or — Marx forbid! — to pray.

Parents are to education what blacks are to civil rights: indispensable hand puppets, whose importance should always be proclaimed even as, in practice, the role of those who actually live with the consequences of Poor Lenin must be mashed into the thinnest layer of insignificance, presenting with such gratifying awards as "Tallest Midget in the Circus."

Real roles for parents open a Pandora's Box of problems. Pretty soon empowered parents might ask why their kids think President Benjamin Franklin invented Quaker Oats or why America started the Second World War by dropping an atomic bomb on Tokyo (and aren't we also, then, responsible for all those Godzilla attacks during the 1950s?)

Real roles for parents could make everyone re-evaluate the importance of the traditional nuclear family. Poor Lenin knows that this institution is simply a bourgeois patriarchal remnant of America's past, and single mothers, preferably a drug addict with many children from many fathers, are our real hope of Poor Lenin's future America. What is that dream of Poor Lenin? He wants to create a society with no class (and he's just the one who can do it.)

You can't make an omelet without breaking people

Poor Lenin knows that people are just like all the other stuff in his materialistic universe. There is no such thing as personal merit, personal guilt, personal value, or personal rights. We are all just little dolls or small plastic soldiers in Poor Lenin's toy box. He opens his box, brings out his toys, and tries to create a "perfect world" (or at least what today looks like a perfect world.) That means throwing some of the dolls around or smashing some of the plastic soldiers. Because like all of us – except, of course, Poor Lenin himself – are all just things, it is the final product that matters. The end always justifies the means.

So, when Poor Lenin decided that little children of color needed to mix more fully in school with little pink children, he shoved them all onto school buses. They traveled each day for long rides, sometimes lasting an hour or more, to a distant school where they knew no one and where their parents were not part of the neighborhood. The time taken away from study, sleep, and family was replaced by exposure to fear, to monotony, and to sullenness. No matter! Kids are just stuff too! It was the grand goal that mattered.

Did forced busing make children more likely to use drugs? Probably it did. Did it make premarital unprotected sexual relations and teenage pregnancy more likely? Yeah, I guess. Did it cost poor school districts money that could otherwise have been used for educational purposes? Sure. Did it increase traffic congestion, needlessly pollute the air, use fossil fuels, and help wear down the streets of the inner cities? Well, if you care about that sort of thing...I suppose so.

Did middle class families sell their homes at sacrificial prices and move into much more racially segregated areas to spare their children the horror of forced school busing? If you want to get picky, yes. Did it turn the centers of big cities into decaying, crime ridden, war zones, insuring that young black children grew up with little chance of escaping drugs, adolescent procreation, crime, prostitution, and poor educations? All of that is true, but you're missing the point!

Poor Lenin has a grand vision for the future. He will tax people into penury to make our educational system "work." He will create vast empires of social programs to help the destroyed lives of young people recover hope which his social programs wrecked. He will implement draconian environmental regulations to control the very pollution that his forced busing created in the first place. He will rebuild the inner cities, their neighborhoods, and their transportation systems with huge government borrowing (the way it should be done!)

The saddest part of all this, at least to Poor Lenin, is that no one ever thanks him for first shattering their lives and their communities and then recreating it into the image of his Brave New World. The ingrates! It is almost as if these eggs thought that they had a free mind, a private conscience, or – even worse – an immortal soul. Poor Lenin has no illusions about that! The purpose of existence is to make new, increasingly creative, omelets and the reasons for having people at all is so that we have some eggs to crack.

It's not what you know, it's who you bribe

Poor Lenin is bothered by facts, annoyed by reason, and insulted by evidence. Show him the money! While many Americans think government is intended to provide for the common defense, promote the general welfare, and secure the blessings of liberty, Poor Lenin sees through all of that muck! Government is a business operation, just like, well, Al Capone in Chicago. The purpose of any government program, any office of federal, state, or local government, and any elected office is to turn a nice profit for bureaucrats, political bosses, and those who bribe those bosses.

What better place to get money than from the very people who print the money! What better way to turn a profit than to use the "protection" system that the Mafia uses — only do it legally! The silly idea that schools, for example, are intended to teach children can be cast aside pretty quickly once Poor Lenin explains to you just how much money teachers' unions place into the hands of politicians. The very offensive notion that teachers should be tested on their knowledge or that children's progress on standardized tests should be used to adjust teachers' salaries (or — gasp! — that eight layers of administrators and superintendents may not be needed for schools) forgets the most important thing: the NEA and teachers' unions have paid for their right at the trough!

The same is true for almost any social program imaginable or for any pork project. Elected officials are like the checkout clerk at the grocery. Poor Lenin picks out the items he wants out of government and then, after the prices have been determined, he pays the bill and the politicians deliver the goods. While some silly Americans think that money should be made in the free market, Poor Lenin knows that it should be made in the government market.

And, of course, everything that government ever does is covered with the gaudy makeup of noble intentions: so what if programs never seem to do what they were intended? Who suffers, except the voters and taxpayers and other little unimportant people? Those who had paid their admission price get to participate in the show, while the riff-raff stayed outside.

True, in the other fields of human interaction, like business or faith or friendship or art, no one can be forced to participate and so people actually get something for what they invest. But the nice thing (at least, in Poor Lenin's eyes) about government is that it can be an omnipresent monopoly whenever and wherever it decides to operate. If you "own" a piece of the government, rather than having that piece of the government belong to everyone and to no one equally, then you can get whatever you want out of government – and that means "goodies" of every sort: tenured civil service jobs, support for universities that teach propaganda, welfare programs which enslave the poor, anything that helps Poor Lenin and his pals stay in good shape personally. Because, as Poor Lenin knows so well, nothing in government ever really fails; it simply lacks enough funding, enough authority, or enough power.

It is a con as old as the crooked judges condemned by the ancient prophets of Israel, and just as rewarding! Government is not what is just, but what is profitable. It is not what helps and works, but what helps and works for Poor Lenin and his chums. It is not what you, or anyone, actually knows, but whose pockets have been lined and in what way.

Lobbyists infest Washington. Why? The answer is easy. We all know why. If government becomes the easiest, quickest, and best way to wealth and to power and to influence, then it will be placed on the auction table, only without regard to what is best for us. The only thing that will matter is what is best for those who pay to play.

Everybody talks about the weather but only Poor Lenin does anything about It

Weather is one of those reminders from God that "Man, thou art dust and to dust thy shall return." We have been granted by our Creator the ability to control bits and pieces of our lives, but only that. Humans are far closer to being zero than to being infinity. We live on a tiny spinning dot of mud in a vast universe. Some stray asteroid or comet could come to close to our planet without much warning and bring all we have done into ashes all around us. Each day could be our last and the last of our species.

This is not hyperbole nor is it intended to depress, but it is simple, clear, scientific fact. We have only vague speculations on how the universe began and conflicting scientific theories about how it will end. Not only is our ignorance vast, but our influence over our reality is tiny. We will all die (that is one of the first hard facts of life.) Everyone we know and love will die too. The cities we build will one day be gone.

The environment around us is much more powerful than us. The power in a bolt of lighting is exponentially more powerful than nuclear weapons. When volcanoes erupt, then the global atmosphere really does change. When the earth quakes we quake too. It is vast hubris to assume that we can do much at all to affect climate change.

Indeed, the rotation of the earth produces climate change much greater than any global warming guru ever dreamt we could make ourselves, and the revolution of the earth around its sun produces real, predictable, and dramatic climate change. Climate change is not only as natural as anything else in nature, but without climate change it is likely that man would never have developed crops, villages, or technology.

In fact, climate change for a long time was considered so vital to humans that we devised methods to affect how the climate worked. Aztec warriors would capture prisoners and priests would cut out their living hearts. Babies would be sacrificed to gods. Mutilation, murder, and mystery cults all did unspeakable things to control weather. These were based upon the best human knowledge and thought at the time.

Everybody talks about the weather but nobody does anything about it, Mark Twain once opined. Actually, the ancients devoted vast energy and great violence to do something about the weather. Blood flowed, treasuries were emptied, and absurdities were embraced – all to get the weather just right for man.

But, of course, weather – like everything else in our lives except our will to listen to God, to love our fellow man, and to seek truth without fear – is ultimately beyond our power. We can seed clouds and maybe cause a little rain. We can certainly create artificial environments with air conditioning and heating. But do anything about climate change or any other real change in the weather? Poor Lenin and his Aztec priests may think so, but we and our Maker know better. Everybody talks about the weather, but only Poor Lenin really seems to believe that we can do anything much about it.

The bigger they are, the better they are

Poor Lenin loves size. Big government is, almost automatically, good. Big cities are much better than small towns. Big organizations, like the United Nations merit serious consideration no matter how unserious the prattle that comes out of it. The federal government is always more noble than state governments. Giant educational systems that seem to swallow up students are good to Poor Lenin. One World Government, of course, is the dream that would make Poor Lenin weep with joy.

This love of bigness, however, goes beyond just government. Although Poor Lenin loves to pretend to champion the little guy against the big corporation, actually Poor Lenin finds big corporations much better than small businesses. Why? Big corporations set up vast internal bureaucracies. Each new government edict, each new item of the agenda of "social responsibility," each demand of a giant labor union – all these require an enormous number of paper pushers, pubic relations staffers, lawyers, and other unproductive people.

When things are small, then the individual tends to stick out as himself and not as a member of this group or that or as a functionary for some huge program or policy. Merit counts more when the number of players is small.

People in neighborhoods tend to know each other. Folks who work in small businesses quickly size up just who the other people in the business are.

Poor Lenin always thinks in terms of the "masses" or "the people," and almost never in terms of this man or that woman. Poor Lenin is attracted to politics specifically because it tends to marinate individuality in a strong flavor of partisanship. The spirit of partisanship, especially when the party has a position on almost everything, gives Poor Lenin a feeling of belonging, a submersion of conscience, an abandoned soul, a united mind – the mind of Big Brother – which trumps every human feeling or belief. God gave us a soul and free will, and yet, through the bigness of Babel, Poor Lenin wants to give this soul back to God.

The "front," the "united," the "union," the "national," the "common" – these are the words which Poor Lenin loves to us to describe any human activity. Simple size can swallow almost anything good and turn it into mush. The small business, the family home, the individual spirit are all anathema to Poor Lenin. Big is better. Big crushes the person into the madness of the crowd. Big is Hitler speaking for hours to entranced Germans, with searchlights panning the night skies, consuming each private thought and each decent impulse. Big is the federal government and its vast labyrinth in which no certainty can exist except the certainty of the throng.

THE BIGGER THEY ARE, THE BETTER THEY ARE

The smallness of the individual, of the family, of the little business, of the church or synagogue, of the neighborhood – these small communities of private life, which respond quickly to reality and which can be grasped by each of us, these are poison to Poor Lenin. The Bigger They Are, to Poor Lenin, the Better They Are: big enough to swallow us alive.

The end justifies the meanness

Poor Lenin, like all Marxists and like all Nazis, believes that the end justifies any tactic. Lying, hiding facts, destroying personal reputations, making promises that you have no intention of keeping – all of these are perfectly fine to Poor Lenin. The party, the movement, the cause – that is the only good in life. Poor Lenin never questions it. He firmly believes that he and his co-partisans have a plan which, given time, will end the problems of the world (or so he tells himself, anyway, until he finally believes it.)

There are many problems with this sort of pseudo-thinking, but the biggest problem is this: We can never truly know the final consequences of our actions. This is true no matter how noble the end may seem. Consider a truly ghastly goal – Hitler's plan to murder all of European Jewry. In his mind, this was a moral goal. So, to Hitler shoving human beings into cattle cars and then exterminating by poisonous gas millions of men, women, and children was morally tolerable because the goal was (in his vile thinking) moral. He believed, as the Bolsheviks believed in the liquidation of the Kulak class, that a final goal which could be deemed "good" meant using tactics that included cold blooded murder, terrorism, vicious lies, and other evil means could be justified.

The problem is not just that the utopia predicted never is benign. We mortals can never predict the consequences of our actions. What were the consequences of the Holocaust? Jews all over the world, who often disagreed about almost everything, very quickly agreed on one thing: Never again! The impetus for creating the State of Israel had moved very slowly before the Shoah. After the war ended, this slight wind became a hurricane of political will. If Hitler had not murdered the Jews, if he had not driven the small number of Jews out of Germany, if he had stopped somewhat short of his geopolitical aims, then perhaps, today, he would be revered as a German statesman and his hatred of Jews simply a footnote in his political biography.

If King George III had been less obstinate, then perhaps the United States would never have been born, and the British Empire would have grown into a sort of dotty patchwork with unclear values, and the world would have been deprived of the Declaration of Independence or the Gettysburg Address. Who knows? We don't (and that is for sure.)

Our powers to see the future are very lame. One pilot in the Pacific Theater in mid-1942 near Midway, on a hunch, flew over one cloud bank and within a few hours four Japanese fleet carriers were sunk and the entire course of the Second World War was changed. Our lives are filled with unpredictable consequences and unintended effects. What can we control? A prophet in Ancient Israel gave us all the guidance we need or that we can acquire: "Do justice. Love mercy. Walk humbly with your Lord."

Poor Lenin hates to hear this, but almost nothing in life is really in our hands. We are microbes to the Almighty. We live. In a nanosecond of cosmic time, we die. Whatever lofty goals, whatever dreams of dialectical materialism we fancy, whatever schemes we devise for perfecting humanity, we have no power – or almost no power – really to do anything.

This does not trouble people who feel themselves in the palm of a Loving Creator, but to people like Poor Lenin, who see themselves as petty gods and little goddesses, this is a distant, unendurable horror. Because for Poor Lenin, the End – the grand plan he thinks reality needs – justifies the Mean, the meanness, the breaking of the rules, and the crimes of every other small time crook.

Look out for the union label

Labor unions once did some good. Under the principled leadership of men like Samuel Gompers, voluntary associations of workers organized for the improvement of working conditions and wages honestly and fairly. Unlike in other nations, American labor unions did not become a political party. This did not mean that there was no conflict between labor and management, but it meant that the arguments were economic, not political or legal.

Later, labor unions evolved into organizations that engaged more in political campaigning than in collective bargaining. This fit more into the plans of Poor Lenin, who favors compulsion over choice. In a famous 1988 legal case, *Communications Workers v. Beck*, the Supreme Court ruled that a union worker could not be compelled to pay union dues which were going to be used just for political purposes. As it turned out in that case, most union dues were used to run campaign ads, collect voting rolls, send out literature to members and so forth. Forcing someone, as a condition of employment, to contribute to a political party he opposed was unconstitutional. Unions almost never tell workers about these constitutional rights and intimidate in all sorts of ways members who get in the way of union bosses. The miserable connection of organized crime with labor unions is just another sad legacy of an honorable association corrupted by political power.

Nevertheless, until a few decades ago, there was good in labor unions. Most members, like steelworkers, auto workers, and miners, did work that America needed. Union members produced a great deal of the industrial wealth of our country. And although the AFL-CIO was a virtual appendage of the Democrat Party, leaders like George Meany and Lane Kirkland were strong anti-Communists. The record of labor unions helping Solidarity in Poland, for example, was real and important. Poor Lenin, however, has outlasted men like Meany and imposed his totalitarian vision on labor unions.

The bureaucracies of many labor unions have become infested with Nazi Brownshirts. When Newt Gingrich ended 46 years of one party rule in the House of Representatives, union thugs tried to bully and harass his office. Most labor union members these days are public employees, and one of the earliest and strongest established principles of trade unionism was that public employees cannot legally or morally form a union.

One consequence is that public schools, because of the NEA and related goon squads, have effectively destroyed the public school system and at the same time kept political leaders from allowing the poor and middle class a real option, except home schooling. The crass partisanship of the NEA has also led to ridiculously offensive ideological indoctrination in many schools, the extinguishment of moral education, and a host of other plagues which in a school system run by parents or serious educators would not exist.

Increasingly union hirelings – political employees – behave like thugs in open forums for political discussion. When our industrial base is crumbling, once patriotic unions simply demand, politically, that government run businesses (as companies go bankrupt) and that taxpayers effectively pay the ridiculous compensation and benefit packages which broke the private firms.

Ads once ran asking consumers to "Look for the union label" as a way of encouraging good hearted Americans to help their fellow countrymen who were working at honest and serious jobs. Now, to any morally or intellectually serious patriot, the warning about almost anything that labor unions do is this: "Look out for the union label."

Mein Kampus

There was a time, not too many decades ago, when the New Left went on a rampage on college campuses. The Berkley Free Speech Movement demanded such vital intellectual prerogatives as the right of students to scream obscenities on the commons or to sleep with whomever they wished. America (or Amerika) was vilified as a fascist nation in speech after speech (the idiocy of armies of unpleasant people being able day after day to screech in public against the government in a fascist state was obvious to everyone but these students.) Poor Lenin was at the heart of these antics, as he was on the quieter underground assault on academia.

This assault began many decades ago. In the 1920s and 1930s, academics began to plant seeds in developing minds: human life is perfectible (if you break a few eggs without remorse); progress is good (we are, the Prophet Marx declared, confirmed by St. Darwin, moving towards a better future); morality is relative (and relatively unimportant); truth is just opinion. This is not something which only happened in Amerika. Students were at the forefront of the National Socialist movement. Soviet students were compelled to study and recite the cant of communism.

Professors and administrators, during the 1960s, were presented often as opponents or victims of student agitation. This was seldom true. Professors were apologists for Stalin and the Soviet Union; they presented totalitarian communism as simply "an alternative view" of the world; professors pretended to be shocked by the demonic radicalism of student agitators, but quietly nodded noting that "they understood" the core causes of discontent.

In fact, the bureaucrats of academia were totalitarians as thuggish as any nicely dressed, well-mannered government official in Nazi Germany. They crushed all opposition within the university environment. Forty years ago, writers were noting that thinkers who endorsed ideas like strong anti-communism or market economies were almost never invited to speak at college campuses. Faculty organizations and collegial associations in various disciplines adopted positions that were positively Orwellian in their inherent dishonesty and bias.

Now history, political science, philosophy, and psychology departments at colleges are vast wastelands of Leftist drivel. The different dogmas of the Left have become entrenched as iron totalitarian law in other fields of study. Homosexuality, thus, is "normal" whether it is or not. The planet is warming, whether it is or not. Men and women have the exact same abilities, whether they do or not. Evolution by natural selection has moved from Darwin's Theory to Darwin's Law.

MEIN KAMPUS

Free expression is openly punished. Campuses have become little Maoist party cells, in which whatever Poor Lenin says is exalted in the Little Red College Textbook and whatever Poor Lenin opposes is not even open for consideration or discussion. Grades are determined based upon orthodoxy, academic positions are given and advancement depends upon absolute adherence to the majority consensus (which, of course, has been pre-determined by decades of ideologically inspired administrative decisions.) It is no longer our campus, but rather, to Poor Lenin, it is Mein Kampus, a Nazified, closed collective mind.

Dreaming about the girl next whore

Once it was the dream of every young man to marry the nice girl, the pretty pig-tailed girl next door, who slowly blossomed into something beautiful – and innocent. Girls, too, once treasured their innocence, their virginity, their privacy. We – normal people and not sociopaths – encouraged this. Sure, young men want to see disrobed young women; yes, young men have lurid fantasies as well. This is as old and as natural as nature.

But society understood that it was in everyone's interest to regulate these hormonal impulses by systems of conscious self control. Once dances and other social events were constructed and monitored by adults who – contrary to teenagers' belief – recalled exactly what it was like to be young. For everyone's sake, sexual promiscuity, explicit pornography, and giving free reign to every adolescent impulse were understood to have very destructive long term consequences.

But that is exactly what Poor Lenin wants. The more long term destructive consequences, the better! Young ladies who become young whores or young trollops soon become dependent upon structures other than family. They become welfare moms or crack whores or Vegas strippers. Moreover, young people are told by Poor Lenin that any control of their raging hormones is unnatural.

So, if you like the girl next door, if you kind-of-pretty-much-plan-to-marry the girl next door, or at least to live with her for a few years, and then form a "serious relationship," then, well, do it! What's the worst that can happen? (Well, other than incurable venereal disease, unwanted pregnancy, abortion, heart-broken parents and families, lethal sicknesses like AIDS, long term psychological problems and, well, that sort of "stuff"?)

Brides wear white most of the time because someone expects them to wear white and not because it once symbolized the chastity and virginity of the bride. The special intimacy of sexual intercourse, once a private and cherished bond between husband and wife, has been turned instead into a pornographic exhibition and an accepted system of premarital relations located somewhere between dating and informal adolescent brothels.

The girl next door, in tragically large numbers, has become the whore next door. Poor Lenin has done nothing to stop this, and he insists that no one else do anything either. As with abortion, Poor Lenin insists that those who warn young ladies that the life of the prostitute is grim and that visits to abortionists are even grimmer, are busy-bodies trying to impose Judeo-Christian values on us (which, of course, Poor Lenin considers a horror.)

The fact that premarital virginity has been prized throughout the history of civilization is blithely ignored as irrelevant. The girl next door, who is now the whore next door, is to Poor Lenin just another type of animal in nature.

The National Council of Churchless

Poor Lenin does not hate organized religion. He hates organized religion that he does not control. As with all other areas of public life, as with the Mafia and the little shop on the street, Poor Lenin is not so much opposed to organized religion as he is opposed to organized religion which he and his pals do not run for their benefit and for the confusion and demoralization of everyone else.

Ordinary people, those of us who believe in what they profess and who do not lie about who they are, are astounded to find that Poor Lenin establishes organizations which are the exact opposite of what they profess to be. So, the ACLU is a staunch opponent of real civil liberties and instead fights for the power of the state and of the politically correct to increase. A Christian student in public school has the "right" to listen to the anti-Christian harangues of Poor Lenin's school teachers. He does not have the right to be home schooled or to celebrate his faith in public schools. The pregnant girl has the "right" to have some strange doctor murder her baby, but does not have the right to be fully informed about the risks and dangers of that decision.

Front organizations abound in Poor Lenin's world. The AARP supports anything that Poor Lenin wants, because its function is not to help retired persons at all, but simply and solely to advance the agenda of Poor Lenin. Likewise the AFL-CIO stands athwart the real interests of working Americans by supporting a green agenda, opposing drilling for oil where oil lies in America, and the American Medical Association prostitutes itself before the Holy Grail of Socialized Medicine.

Why, then, is anyone surprised that Poor Lenin finds churchmen who are anything but Christians? Organizations like the National Council of Churches do not bother with things like Christian faith, the Gospels, or the traditional beliefs of ordinary Christians. Instead it supports atheistic torturers like Fidel Castro and cauldrons of anti-Christian propaganda like public universities. Why assume that Poor Lenin would not eagerly go to a politically correct divinity school or open a putative "Christian" church as nothing more than a vehicle for his ideological agenda?

Poor Lenin considers nothing sacred at all except power (people who think murdering babies for fun and for profit is fine often have that sort of worldview.) If getting power, getting money, getting attention, and advancing his agenda can come from connection with some church, Poor Lenin will do it in a nanosecond. His pals often conveniently forget that the mingling of religion and politics was not begun by conservatives, but rather by radical clergy who connected their agenda with Christianity.

The problem Poor Lenin had with the "Religious Right" is the same that it had with conservative talk radio: as long as only Poor Lenin and his pals used religion or the media to anoint and to advance their agenda, then these were perfectly proper vehicles, but as soon as others express contrary opinions, then churches become a danger to democracy. The plain fact is this: Poor Lenin will use anything at all to get power, and that includes the prostitution of his soul in an indifferent profession of religious belief.

That's Entertainment????

Once television shows presented a happy picture of America. Humor on the screen was the humor of life itself, as old as Aristophanes and Moliere and as American as Mark Twain or Will Rogers. It was seldom obscene or profane and it was not based upon social conspiracy theories of parents oppressing children, husbands oppressing wives, rich oppressing poor, and so forth.

Once television and cinema found hilarity in life without also finding nihilistic grimness. Families watched programs that found fun in the human condition without exposing exploitation of some humans at the expense of others. When Americans watched I Love Lucy or The Honeymooners, they saw ordinary people living happy, but imperfect, lives. It entertained rather than harangued.

Romance was once…romantic. Men and women, boys and girls, went through all the angst, the allure, the amorousness, and apprehension that is part of romantic love. Villains were rare and always ran afoul of the unwritten rules of romantic theater: the good guys and good gals win. Sexuality was always present, but it was seldom explicit and never mimicked the mind-numbing explicitness of pornography. Sexual tension lay behind unopened doors and it was much more powerful for all that.

Drama and action and grand themes were present in film, radio, books, and television as well, but these were played out by bigger than life figures rather than little marms and punks. The Hunchback of Notre Dame, for example, was truly tragic, but also truly inspirational. Sergeant York was shown, as a real life hero, with dashes of fiction but without disillusioning and invented flaws.

What of entertainment generally? At one time entertainers could act, sing, dance, mime, play piano (or some musical instrument), and joke. Their profession was entertainment, and that meant versatility and talent. Will Rogers began his career twirling a lasso. Jack Benny played the violin. Entertainers were expected to engage in variety, and they did.

What was missing, of course, was "the message." Now we are drowning in something which pretends to be entertainment, but which is, in fact, nothing more than the message of Poor Lenin dressed up in a thousand different ways. Because message entertainment is the only entertainment allowed, there is almost no real entertainment, no genuine recreation, for the individual left.

Films, lacking any true novelty, are all too often remakes and these remakes are all too often simply transform an entertaining old film into new, boring film which sates the lust of Poor Lenin to enter every crevice of our waking thoughts. The greatest object of our true entertainment, a studied, even-handed, and honest examination of the human condition, has been replaced by a straitjacket of Poor

THAT'S ENTERTAINMENT????

Lenin's invention. Small wonder, then, that our children are glued to video games or text each other all the time. We lack the common glue which was once Hollywood or radio or television. Our children already know what it is like to hear Poor Lenin's monotonous message all the time at school, in media, even in commercials. They yearn for what they do not have and what we do not have either: true entertainment.

We have nothing to fear but freedom Itself

Franklin Roosevelt began the process of morphing the foundational principles of the Republic into odd curiosities. "Life, liberty, and the pursuit of happiness," so classically enshrined in the language of the Declaration of Independence, is summed up often as simply "freedom." FDR was a big fan of freedom…sort of. He just had a problem with prepositions. So, he would not believe so much in the right of pursuit of happiness as something like "freedom from unhappiness." FDR kept confusing "from" with "of." The essence of freedom is the right to make mistakes, the right to be miserable, the right – as Jews and Christians believe – to even reject the love of the Blessed Creator.

Freedom is the catalyst through which all good and enlightened human action occurs. If we are not free, then we may be forcibly prevented from doing some bad things, but we are also almost incapable of doing any good things. But Poor Lenin does not want us doing anything which could be counted on its own as good or bad. What Poor Lenin wants is to have us as his animals, his herd, and his livestock.

Slaves, like livestock, are not necessarily mistreated. They are simply treated as if they had no independent consciousness, conscience, or soul. They have "freedom from want" and "freedom from harm." Because they are the owned possession of Poor Lenin, he has no interest in seeing them starved or be slaughtered, unless that suits his purposes.

Real Freedom – "freedom of" – includes the chance of personal failure as well as personal success. With real freedom, the decision making devolves to the smallest place that it can, our own free will. Just as all life ends in death, freedom is a guarantee of nothing, except the almost certainty that free men and women will often make mistakes. On balance, the virtues of freedom insist, the individual is a better judge of his own best interests than any remote collective leadership.

Poor Lenin does not see the world that way. He knows best. If every problem in the world is a nail (and Poor Lenin thinks that it is) then every solution in the world is a bigger hammer. Give more and more and more power over our lives to Poor Lenin, surrender more and more and more of our own free choices to Poor Lenin, and he will be able to deliver us through more "freedoms' from."

This includes inverse freedoms which FDR never imagined: Freedom from worry, freedom from family, freedom from work, freedom from religion, freedom from sin, freedom from truth, freedom from knowledge, and the like. Each negation of any personal value is the addition of a new freedom from for Poor Lenin.

WE HAVE NOTHING TO FEAR BUT FREEDOM ITSELF

His penchant for freedom from means that any federal program must be scripted ahead of time and thought out by bureaucrats, regulators, legislators and their staffers long before these freedoms "protected" by the program are tested against the reality of ordinary life. It is impossible, therefore, for any program intended to strip us of freedom and protect us in a smothering womb of total control to ever fail. While Poor Lenin luxuriates in pseudo-freedom, he cannot abide real freedom. He believes, sincerely, that all we have to fear is freedom itself.

All speech is free, but some speech is more free than others

Poor Lenin loves to tout his absolute support for freedom of speech – actually, he calls it freedom of expression, because that allows him to have freedom apply to showing playboy playmates as well. Freedom of speech in America means the right to advocate the destruction of that very freedom of speech in America. It means the right of the Leftist media to mislead us or to outright lie to us. But some speech, in Poor Lenin's world, is more free than others.

If a union is voted in by 51% of the members of a shop, for example, the 49% lose their right to express opinions openly on collective bargaining. If a television network corporation presents facts incorrectly, that is free speech. If a corporation advertising on that network presents facts incorrectly, that is punishable "misleading advertising." If a member of a racial minority viciously calls a white person some offensive name, that is First Amendment expression. If a white person does the same to a member of a minority, that is hate speech.

Just as the only "discrimination" outlawed by Poor Lenin is the discrimination of certain classes of Americans against other classes of Americans (whites against blacks, men against women, heterosexuals against homosexuals,

Christians against Moslems), the only freedom allowed in expression is the freedom of those who support what Poor Lenin says or writes or performs.

Forty years of monopolistic, biased network news reporting which favored Poor Lenin was so absolutely constitutionally guaranteed that even talking about the need for balance in network television news was infringing upon the constitutional rights of massive and powerful corporations who own the networks. Now, a handful of radio shows, only on the air for a few hours a day but opposing the agenda of Poor Lenin require bureaucratically enforced "balance."

Who will decide what is "balance"? Certainly it will not be the people casting economic ballots in the marketplace. Sure, listeners have a dial which allows them to hear dozens of different radio programming or AM or FM, but Poor Lenin does not trust the people to choose what is best for them (they might decide that Poor Lenin and his cronies were not friends of the people but rather parasitical nags!) So fairness will have to be decided by the right people – faceless bureaucrats hidden in the bowels of some obscure part of the federal government, residing in the hermetically sealed bubble of Washington, D.C., and making purely subjective judgments using tools which solemnly profess to be objective.

Expression is the right of those who have ideas and opinions which agree with Poor Lenin to propagate those biases. Fifty years ago, students had the right to attack the political views of their professors. Now, they do not. What has changed? The professors fifty years ago were "wrong" and the students "right," while today some students might question the doctrinaire Marxism which is pandemic in academia. Forty years ago, a free press which attacked federal political leaders was evidence of a robust democracy. Now it is evidence of a rogue and dangerous media, undermining confidence in our government. All Speech is Equal, But Some Speech is More Equal than Others. Thus Saith Poor Lenin.

The UN – United Nazis

Few failures in world politics have been as utterly dismal as the United Nations or, rather, the United Nazis. The term "United Nations" was used to describe those powers that fought together in the Second World War to defeat the Nazis, the Fascists, and the Japanese. The idea was based, very roughly, upon the League of Nations, which failed utterly to prevent aggression, crimes against humanity, rise of totalitarianism, or much of anything else. Before the League of Nations, before the First World War, President Taft proposed an organization of nations which would allow for talking before fighting. In 1911, that made sense. The Great War, as it was long called, might have been prevented if Austro-Hungary knew that Russia would defend Serbia or if France knew that Germany would stand by Austro-Hungary or if Germany knew that Britain would fight to protect France.

In the chaos that followed the First World War, however, no forum for preventing war was going to work. The Bolsheviks were intent on Marxist revolution and worked to disrupt democracies around the world (if the German Communists had really made stopping Hitler their main objective, he would never have gained power – they, in fact, wanted Hitler to become Chancellor of Germany in 1933.) The Japanese were outraged by the meager rewards they received for being a faithful ally, and so were the Italians, who soon turned to Mussolini and Fascism. And no German political leader could ever have accepted the Treaty of Versailles.

Fair treatment of Germany in the 1920s might well have preserved the Weimar Republic. Firm opposition to the horror of Bolshevism might have led to its collapse during the grim years of Stalin's Ukrainian genocide. Fair and firm treatment of Japan might have kept that nation what it was at the end of the First World War: an allied power which fought beside the Americans, British, French, and Italians.

If a League of Nations was a silly idea in the 1920s, a United Nations was a patently absurd idea in the late 1940s. The Soviets had been effective allies of Hitler for much of the Second World War, and it was Hitler who attacked Stalin and not the other way around. The first Secretary General of the United Nations was Alger Hiss, a Soviet agent in the Roosevelt Administration. The Soviet Union was given three votes in the General Assembly (one for Russia, one for Ukraine, and one for Byelorussia), although every other nation had only one vote. The only real opposition that the United Nations has provided to any aggression was in the Korean War, and that was only because the Soviets had boycotted the Security Council.

The United Nations has been conspicuous by its failure to achieve any sort of peace in the Middle East or on the Indian subcontinent or in Africa or in Asia. It has failed utterly to support human rights and has, instead, provided a fig leaf of cover for the most brutal dictatorships imaginable. Think of Adolph Hitler addressing the General Assembly, to general praise, or Nazi Germany having a seat on the Human Rights Council and you have an excellent picture of just what the United Nations (or United Nazis) represents.

But this is not a problem for Poor Lenin. Real freedom terrifies him. Genuine peace is at odds with his love of constant conflict, unless, of course, the peace is enforced by secret police, strict state censorship, and concentration camps. The men who send delegates to the United Nazis and whose delegates control the operation of the United Nazis are virtually indistinguishable from Hitler, Mussolini, Tojo, and all the other baddies of the Twentieth Century.

.

If it ain't broke – break It

Americans have the best health care system in the world. People travel to America from all over the world to get treatment in America which cannot be obtained anywhere else while few, if any, Americans travel to Canada or to Europe to get medical care. That ought to tell us something. And, to Poor Lenin, it does: Let's become just like the Canadians and Europeans! American private health care is the envy of the world. The principal problems with it are avaricious trial lawyers and excessive government regulations (but in Poor Lenin's world, those two conditions can never, ever, be real "problems" and reducing either can never, ever, even be contemplated.)

Beyond just private health care, Americans are incredibly generous in supporting medical charities. Our nation has entire hospitals supported only by private donations to provide, at no cost, care for children, for burn victims, and for countless other people with profound medical problems. Medical research is carried out by foundations established entirely with the free gifts of open hearted Americans to cure nearly every conceivable problem.

Support groups which help people with chronic problems, like Alcoholics Anonymous, are creatures of the American heart and mind and save lives at no cost to the taxpayer and without any government regulation all the time. Churches and synagogues routinely make thoughtful and generous donations to help congregants or the poor or those with extraordinary needs and do so without the slightest push from government.

For those interested in healing the sick, caring for the infirm, finding cures for maladies, and assisting those with extraordinary medical problems, the American system of private doctors, charitable Americans, and free markets is hard to beat. Moreover, for anyone who will listen, the sixty year British experiment with socialized medicine is a flop, producing decades of horror stories topped off with a giant scoop of official, bureaucratic indifference to the fear, pain, and mortality of its subjects, the British people.

The American health care system is not perfect – no health care system can be – but it is hardly broken. Virtually everyone dies. That is the condition of life. But even "imperfections" which are inherent in life can, Poor Lenin believes, be solved by government. Any system that ever fails can be improved through more laws, bureaucracies, regulations, court rulings, and awareness campaigns.

So a health care system in which patients die, medical errors are sometimes made, and in which medical care has a real, rather than an imaginary cost, is not necessarily broken to ordinary Americans. We all know that a car that needs gas in its tank, oil changes, and other periodical maintenance is not broken, but Poor Left would still "fix" it.

April 15...a day that will live in Infamy

April 15th is the day that Americans must file income tax returns. Once, not too many decades ago, Americans had to work until sometime around mid-April just to earn the income necessary to pay their federal income taxes. Each year, this day of freedom (the day of the year in which the average American can begin working for himself, instead of the federal government) comes later in the year.

About thirty-five percent of our national income is gobbled up by government each year. In spite of that, the federal government still runs a huge deficit (which will have to be paid in higher taxes or lower dollar value.) All of that is fine with Poor Lenin, who believes the state should really have everything. Most working Americans never see, until they file their IRS 1040, just how much of what they earn goes to government. "Withholding" is the procedure by which government takes your taxes out ahead of time, does not pay you interest on that money, and allows itself the luxury of giving millions of taxpayers each year "refunds," which are viewed by the gullible as gifts from a benevolent government.

The income tax and particularly the withholding of taxes has created an insidious mechanism through which vast amounts of what Americans produce is gobbled up by a federal as well as state and local governments which simply spend without thought to economy, value, or harm to the taxpayer. It differs from protection money paid to the Mafia, because government purports to give you back something in return which is more than simply keeping the taxpayer out of jail. It is "clean" protection money.

Yet those functions of government which benefit us all are tiny. The Department of Defense, which once was the biggest department of government, is now smaller than the Department of Health, Education, and Welfare. Spending for building and maintaining public roads is a small sliver of government spending. Moreover, road and highways, like utilities run by government, are paid for by the consumer of the services through tolls and utility bills.

Often we taxpayers are compelled to pay for "services" which we consider profoundly against our own interest. Public art is often obscene, profane and mediocre. Public schools, which insist on a stranglehold on the education of our children, are increasingly Poor Lenin's favorite tool of indoctrination – and turn out students who cannot read, write, perform math, grasp history, or have any objective understanding of our government (but, other than that...)

What Poor Lenin does with the federal government, which can just print money, is even worse than what he does with state and local governments, which cannot just print money. The federal tax burden, when the national debt is included, is much deeper into the year than just April 15. In fact, if American taxpayers intended to pay off the national debt, it would take a long time of working for nothing but that purpose to pay it off. Just the interest on the national debt, which must be paid to maintain the integrity of the dollar, takes a huge chunk of tax dollars each year.

How did we get into this mess? There came a point in which Poor Lenin began to borrow to pay for government services instead of taxing enough to pay for the services. (This had the neat advantage, to Poor Lenin, of allowing him to spend like crazy without concern about how this debt with be paid off or even serviced.) Just as important is the sleight of hand trick of federal (and state) withholding, which allows government to conceal from you what you never get to have, your whole paycheck. Blame it on April 15th, a day that will live in infamy.

-

Bless the beasts but not the children

The rights of animals against cruelty are legitimate: Anyone who enjoys the suffering of any living creature is morally flawed. But there is a vast difference between torture and killing. There is also a vast difference between interspecies killing and homicide. Nature mandates that many creatures live by killing. Dogs and cats, for example, cannot survive in their natural state without murdering other living creatures. Sharks, dolphins, whales and other favorites of animal rights activists, also live by the sword (or the tooth and the claw.)

There are higher animal life forms which need not live by killing in the world – primates and bears, for example – and there are a few higher forms of animals who live as vegetarians, like elephants. Nevertheless, stalking, injuring, executing, and consuming other animals is the way of life for many higher levels of animals. Christians and Jews believe that God gave man dominion over the other animals, but even removing religion, there is no doubt that Nature views hunting, killing, and eating the dead as perfectly okay.

Our idea that the treatment of all life should be different from hunting and killing comes from the metaphysical systems of man, not from Nature. So we speak, in the

Bible, of the lamb lying down with the lion – it is a sure bet that neither of those animals thought in such terms.

And animals do not have human notions of compassion. No animal is repelled by the slow, agonizing death of another animal. Dogs, creatures we perceive as gentle and loving, will hunt in packs and tear prey to bits. Cats, another beloved creature, play with their prey before killing them. Some animals kill quickly and others do not, but compassion has no role to play in the method of murder.

People view the pain of other animals quite differently. Those who cannot empathize with suffering animals are considered mentally disturbed or morally debauched. Man, alone, passes laws to control behavior and establishes norms for moral and immoral actions. This has long related to animals, as well as humans. The Kosher killing of animals, for example, is imbued with religious and moral commandments. Calculated by religious tradition or by God or by both, Kosher killing minimizes pain. In Judaism, even the way that we end the life of animals so that we may have food is regulated.

Animals do, however, care for their young. Dogs and cats will fight and even die to protect their offspring. Bears and elephants will do the same. Indeed, we consider it a sign of the dawning of moral purpose when we find animals that show concern, exhibit protection, and perhaps feel affection for their babies. But Poor Lenin does not treat human babies the way animals treat their young. The right to murder, even murder by means which would be prohibited by Poor Lenin if done to heinous murderers, is sacrosanct to Poor Lenin.

We should bless the beast but not the children, in Poor Lenin's perverse moral order. So while Poor Lenin can shed tears for hens in a coop, he cannot muster the slightest emotional pain at a human baby being tortured to death by medical professionals in the womb of a mother, and is probably willing to extend that low status as well to new born babies who are, somehow, unwanted.

What would Poor Lenin say if he found a woman who got pregnant just for the sickening high of being able to murder the baby within her? Nature suggests that this would be rare, but in an age in which Poor Lenin views each abnormality of nature as good and healthy, could anyone rule it out? What if the mother deliberately wanted the baby to die by the most painful type of abortion? All of us now view that sort of diabolical behavior as beyond the pale, but Poor Lenin is always looking for new ways to destroy timeless standards. Some day, perhaps, the only form of cruelty to animals permitted by Poor Lenin will be cruelty to innocent human babies. That is how far we have fallen.

Eating the goose that laid the golden egg

America invented general prosperity. Industrious individuals, hard-working family farms, inventors and innovators, all kissed with the blessing of liberty – these have made not just some Americans but nearly all Americans affluent by any standard of the world or any standard of history. Americans have long been able to become wealthy, if they would just work hard enough, play by the rules, and be patient.

Immigrant families rose, often in a single generation, from wide eyed, impoverished wonder at the miracle of America to being the new leaders of business in America. The chance of self-improvement, the hope of providing a better life for one's children, the opportunity to reach as far as one could grasp – these are the true wealth of America.

And this very hope is the bane of Poor Lenin: how can people be forced to depend upon him when they can just as easily depend upon themselves? The goose that laid the golden egg, the source of American prosperity and also of American individualism, must be killed, cooked, and eaten.

Poor Lenin understands, of course, that as soon as the goose that laid the golden egg is killed, the wealth of America will dry up. That is the idea. A robust middle class of self-reliant, happy, people provides far too much self-assurance for Poor Lenin. He wants America to be like some dreary, slowing dying nation in Europe. Poor Lenin will find use for the meat of the goose. He will listen, as if he cared, to warnings about the horrific mal-investment of killing and eating the goose that lays the golden eggs.

Even if there was no meat on the goose at all, Poor Lenin would want to kill it. How does he execute the source of prosperity? Poor Lenin likes the "death of a thousand cuts." So he introduces ridiculous "job safety" rules, which make the goose get thinner. He imposes regulations on almost everything the goose does, rather like the Nazis first regulated Jews to death before they murdered them. Wherever the goose looks, there are new hedges, new fences, new stop lights.

It does not matter if these obstructions and mine fields do nothing good, nothing good at all, for society. The purpose of these obstructions is to cripple and then to kill the goose. The less the American economy grows, the more ordinary citizens will be compelled to rely on the handouts of Poor Lenin, who has taken this wealth from productive Americans. In the eyes of Poor Lenin, this is a "win-win" situation: the number of Americans who can succeed on their own, and so can be threats to the power of Poor Lenin, will be reduced and the number of Americans who are helpless without the Marxist redistribution of wealth will grow, which means more votes. Killing, cooking, and eating the goose that laid the golden eggs is just what Poor Lenin has on his menu.

I have a nightmare

Martin Luther King Jr. gave a speech almost fifty years ago which touched the hearts of Republicans and Democrats, conservatives and liberals, Jews and Christians, blacks and whites. It was simplicity itself. Reverend King, calling upon Christian love rather than atheistic socialism, said: "Darkness cannot drive out darkness; only light can do that. Hate cannot drive out hate; only love can do that" Dr. King said it and he was right. He also said "I have decided to stick with love. Hate is too great a burden to bear." The love he spoke of was not love based upon race, but rather upon us all being children of a loving God.

He could not have imagined that a movement he championed would be twisted over time into a full-time profession whose managers would insist that "God damn America" or would assert that young white men on a college Lacrosse team were guilty just because a black woman accused them of a crime or that white people deliberately created crack cocaine addicts among black youths. As he said "Injustice anywhere is a threat to justice everywhere." Dr. King meant injustice to young white men as well as to young black men.

Many white Americans supported the message of Martin Luther King. He did not seem to want to lead a movement just to lead a movement, like Jesse Jackson or Al Sharpton. Instead, Dr. King said "I am not interested in power for power's sake, but I'm interested in power that is moral, that is right and that is good." Martin Luther King did not believe that stealing votes or threatening people so that the "good side" would win was justified "The means we use must be as pure as the ends we seek." Nor did Dr. King think that constantly reliving past grievances accomplished anything at all "Never succumb to the temptation of bitterness."

This moral leadership, not political machinations, led men like Charlton Heston to walk with Martin Luther King in his marches. It led many who have since strongly rejected the "interest politics" of the entrenched, enriched, enraged, and empowered "civil rights" leadership to walk together for awhile with a man whose goodness, despite politics, was as crystal clear as the goodness of Ronald Reagan to Americans. This is not what Poor Lenin wants at all.

The idea that people should be judged by the content of their character rather than the color of their skin runs directly contrary to the goal of the professional bosses of eternally aggrieved groups. Dr. King would have said that the color or race of a person should never be considered on employment applications or college admissions. His "successors" (or, rather, his corrupters) insist that the first thing asked should be race, color, gender, national origin and so forth.

I HAVE A NIGHTMARE

Dr. King had a dream that one day we would all live under the warm sunlight of love, and that love, not hate, should bind us to our common humanity. His perverted pseudo-disciples need hatred to be ingrained in our national existence, suspicion to poison every motive, and all solutions to racial harmony to end, ultimately, in failure. Dr. King had a dream. It was a beautiful dream. The selfish, little souls who followed him have turned his dream into our nightmare.

The rumors of my death have been greatly exaggerated

Poor Lenin wants us all to believe that the spirit of freedom, the sense of the transcendent and sacred, the independence of thought and of action – all these lights of liberty - have been destroyed. Poor Lenin has bought every office and authority that could be bought. He has insinuated himself into every honorable institution that could be turned to his dishonorable ends. He has smeared with muck and slime every person or group which persisted in noble intentions despite his siren songs or his snarling threats.

Hollywood repeats the mantras of Poor Lenin. The establishment media echoes whatever Poor Lenin thinks we should hear. School teachers and professors instruct students that the word of Poor Lenin is sacred scripture. Bureaucrats in a thousand different bureaucracies created to supplicate Poor Lenin and his impious pseudo-church spin red tape like spiders spin web to entrap our consciousness and our consciences in the trap of Poor Lenin.

Poor Lenin has his forces marshaled, his armies arrayed, his strategy planned – but he can only conquer America is if the people surrender. His officers live in isolated colonial offices in Hollywood, Washington, and New York or in strongly garrisoned fortresses in academia. Outside these imperial castles, Poor Lenin is hopelessly outnumbered. Public opinion polls show that even in states like Massachusetts, Vermont, Rhode Island, Hawaii, and New York, more Americans call themselves "conservative" than "liberal." Other polls show that the percentage of Americans who consider themselves "liberal" – despite decades of cradle to grave indoctrination – is pathetically small, less than half the number who consider themselves the much ridiculed and maligned "conservative."

Faith in God is alive and well in America. The percentage of Americans who go to church or to synagogue remains a strong majority of the people and Americans are much more religious than most other industrial democracies. In spite of the *New York Times* declaring almost fifty years ago that "God is dead," He is very much alive in the hearts, minds, and lives of most Americans.

Millions of young men and women, despite Poor Lenin's decades of haranguing America about being an imperialist occupier whose troops despoil nations, enlist in a volunteer military at great sacrifice to themselves, travel to another hemisphere, and risk their lives so that we – including, of course, that ingrate, Poor Lenin – can be safe. Ordinary Americans cherish these heroes and thank them for their sacrifice.

Large percentages of official "victims" like blacks, Hispanics, and women have stopped considering themselves victims and started considering themselves blessed to live in the "Land of the free and the home of the brave." They join the vast ocean of polyglot immigrant groups who long ago grasped that living in America was the greatest blessing imaginable, which is why almost no one ever emigrates out of America (even Hollywood types who promise they will if their candidate does not win the presidency.)

America, land of the faithful followers of a loving Creator, land of opportunity for all, land established upon transcendent principles, is still very much alive as a real nation and as an ideal in the breast of every person who yearns for freedom. Despite Poor Lenin, the "Big Bad Wolf," huffing and puffing, he cannot blow down this house. The rumors of the death of America have been greatly exaggerated.

9 781432 756826